Homoeopathic Remedies

TYPE 2 DIABETES MELLITUS

Mujahid Khan

Diabetes mellitus or simply diabetes, is a metabolic of disorder portrayed by high blood glucose/sugar levels (hyperglycemia) that outcome from imperfections in the body's ability to produce and/or use insulin. We are actually living in the world of uncertainties, which is ever changing from unknown to known, better to best, hypothesis to scientific explanation, and so on. During this process mankind is conceived with many adversities and diseases. One such disease, man cursed on himself through his disordered lifestyle, food habits and stressful livelihood is diabetes mellitus.

Diabetes is the body's inability to utilize glucose appropriately. It presently strikes Americans at the rate of one new case every fifty two seconds, and furthermore 3.2 million lives year worldwide and India positions first in the aggregate number of diabetic patients. It turned into an extraordinary risk to the creating countries as they change on toward the westernized ways of life that underscore on sedentary living and rich food.

Developing countries have region specific cultural, social and economic barriers that will put a person at a high risk. Measurable investigation of this well established beast uncovers the inherited prevalence slanted alongside the ways of life and nourishment propensities. Furthermore, thus this malady never exhibits as diabetes alone, yet with obesity, some psycho affective disorders and hypertension.

Satisfactory treatment of diabetes and also expanded accentuation on circulatory strain control and way of life factors, for example, controlling smoking, keeping and maintaining a healthy bodyweight may improve the condition and decreases the risk of most fore mentioned complications.

It is a condition basically characterized by the dimension of hyperglycaemia offering ascends to danger of microvascular harm (retinopathy, nephropathy and neuropathy). It is connected with diminished future, critical horribleness as a result of explicit diabetes related microvascular inconveniences, extended danger of macrovascular complexities (I.H.D, C.V.D), atherosclerosis and decreased individual fulfillment.

A few pathogenetic forms are engaged with the advancement of diabetes. These incorporate procedures, which wreck the beta cells of the pancreas with subsequent insulin insufficiency and others that outcome in protection from insulin activity. The anomalies of carbohydrate, fat and protein digestion are because of insufficient activity of insulin on target tissues coming about because of harshness or lack of insulin. Diabetes mellitus may give trademark indications, for example, polydipsia, polyphagia, fatigue, polyuria, blurring of vision, and weight reduction. Regularly indications are not serious, or may be absent.

Conventional system of medicine is able to control and prevent the further progression of diabetes mellitus but unable to cure the disease. For this reason systematic clinical study as required for efficacious treatment of diabetes. Keeping this in view this study was undertaken so as to outline a scientific approach that could be applied for homoeopathic treatment of diabetes mellitus.

Reparability of this condition is definitely not an archived truth and the main realized methodology is to control the blood glucose levels, which implies a palliative approach.

Experience says that homeopathy emerges for its successful palliative method of treatment with no difficulties and furthermore diabetes is such an infection which can be drawn closer even without drug just by general administration and lifestyle adaptation.

The current therapeutic framework goes for revising the unsettling influences at receptor level improving the glucose take-up by overseeing drugs relating to it, here comes the components like cost sensitiveness effectiveness, and also drug dependency. So this provides us an opportunity to prove the age old beliefs of homoeopathy in treating chronic diseases using constitutional approach, there by proving homoeopathy to be a better asset in treatment of diseases like diabetes mellitus and also to understand and demonstrate the quality of life and adaptation of a person towards his disease and to his circumstances before and after the treatment confirming the efficacy and holistic nature of our medicine.

Homoeopathic treatment can enhance all dimensions of wellbeing i.e. mental, physical, environmental aspects, and social, not simple annihilation of physical manifestations. This study basically concentrates on chronic disease diabetes because it is upcoming fact of its threat to the society.

Consequently this study is an unassuming attempt to highlight the efficacy of homoeopathic medicines and role of management in the treatment of diabetes mellitus (type II).

Health is the dimension of practical or potentially metabolic productivity of a life from at both the micro (cellular) and macro (social) level. In the therapeutic field, health is usually characterized as a life form's capacity to productively react to difficulties (stressors) and viably reestablish and support a "state of balance", know as homeostasis[1]. Another by and large recognized importance of health is that of the World Health Organization (WHO), which express that "health is a state of finish mental, physical and social thriving and not only the nonappearance of sickness or disease".

Recent years, we keep observing different diseases of the mankind which are altogether nothing but manmade diseases[1], one such disease is diabetes mellitus which has its roots planted deep in the evolution of mankind, irrespective of its mode of affinity and probability we know that it has a combination of heritable and environmental influences acting on it making it more complex not only to understand but also to treat. Adding to these complexes the fast lifestyles adopted by the developing countries adds fire to this burning sweet issue.

WHAT HISTORY SAYS ABOUT DIABETES

As man started in questing about things in and around him he started to know himself better, during of this methods he differentiated normal from abnormal and those abnormal things [diseases] were labeled/classified diversely consistent with their similarities and characteristics. Even though they're named in times current, they were known to mankind from times immemorial as he was and is the victim. Diabetes was known to Egyptians around 3500 prior asclarified in the restorative books of the antiquated Egypt.

Romans understood diabetes through polyuria as they believed flesh and limbs were melting down to urine, this observation came because there is gradual wasting in the patient with diabetes. The Indian physicians named Charaka and Sushrutha, the well known ayurvedic physicians described that the diabetic patients pass sweet urine in large amounts i.e. rain of honey and so they named the disease as Madhumeha[2].

Arabs are another group of observers who came with the opinion that diabetes can complicate with gangrene and it has a hereditary tendencies. Avicenna was the renowned physician who brought such observations in his book Canon of medicine. Even today we call this clinical entity as diabetes mellitus because mellitus refers to honey[3]. In the 2nd century ARATAEEUS AD "OF CAPPADOCIA" coined the diabetes (running through a siphon) [4].

LANDMARKS IN HISTORY OF DIABETES[5]

1500 BC: Ebers papyrus [Egypt] described polyuria and honey urine.

400 BC: Sushrutha in India described sweetness in urine

1674 AD: Thomas wills rediscovered the sweetness in urine.

1784 AD: Mathew Dobson, demonstrated sweetness of urine.

1800 AD: Dietary Regime outlined by rollo for diabetes.

1867 AD: Paul Langerhans described islets of langerhans in pancreas.

1869 AD: Dog is made diabetic by removing pancreas.

1921 AD: Fred Banting orthopedic surgeon isolated insulin and got Nobel Prize.

1922 AD: 14yrs old boy Leonard Thompson in Toronto received 1st insulin injection.

1926 AD: Abel was prepared insulin in crystalline form.

1936 AD: Houssay, hypophysectomy ameliorated diabetes in dogs.

1948 AD: Diabetic Detection drive first done by American Diabetic Association.

1955 AD: First tablet for diabetes introduced structure of insulin detected.

1959 AD: Immunoassay for insulin first done by Berson and yallon.

1960 AD: Sanger was established the amino acid sequence of insulin.

1989 AD: Steiner was discovered pro insulin.

1990 AD: Human insulin prepared by genetic engineering 5 Nobel prizes awarded for that work.

EPIDEMIOLOGY

It is estimated that there will be more than 200 million diabetics within the next 10 years. India has just turn in to the "diabetes capital" of the world with than 3 crores influenced patients, which is a tip of ice self. Despite the fact that type 2 diabetes is a heterogeneous disease, it is by a long short the commonest type, agreeing for relatively 90% of all diabetics. Epidemiological studies report varying prevalence ranging from 0.8% in Nigeria to nearly 18% in Ontario, Canada. The highest rates are seen in some ethnic American tribes, notably the Pima Indians (over 50%). Low prevalence (<3%) is generally found in the least developed rural communities with a low level of obesity. In India, studies have shown a rising predominance of type 2 diabetes mellitus. Prevalence of diabetes is more in urban than in rural areas. Predominance of IGT is also high. Considering the high rate of conversion of IGT to diabetes, this would suggest a further increment in the quantity of diabetes later on. With a rising number of diabetic subjects, the weights of diabetic difficulties are likewise prone to increase. The commonness of disease in grown up was found to be 4.0-11.6% in urban & 2.4% in rural dwellers. High frequencies of IGT, shown by those researches, staring from 3.6-9.1%, show the potential for further ascent in predominance of diabetes mellitus in the coming decades.[4]

WHAT IS DIABETES

Diabetes mellitus is a syndrome of decreased saccharide, fat and supermolecule metabolism caused by either lack of hypoglycemic agent secretion or ablated sensitivity of the tissues to hypoglycemic agent (insulin)[4].

(or)

Diabetes mellitus is a group of metabolic disorder characterized by hyperglycemia mainly resulting from inadequate insulin secretion, insulin action, and insulin resistance [6].

Both the statement tells us that insulin is the culprit so before understanding the diabetes, the anatomical and physiological basis of insulin secretion and function is worth a reading for an easy voyage.

ANATOMICAL BACKGROUND OF DIABETES MELLITUS

The Pancreas[7]

The pancreas (pan = all, kreas = flesh) is a gland that is partly exocrine and partly endocrine. The exocrine component secretes the digestive pancreatic juice; and the endocrine part secrets hormones, e.g. insulin. In addition that pancreas has an important internal secretion is largely responsible for maintaining blood sugar (glucose) levels. It is a soft, prolonged and lobulated organ. Mostly likely explained by the langerhans, which is taken up by the circulation system and in concerned with glucose metabolism i.e. insulin. The normal blood sugar (glucose) level is 70 to 160 milligrams per deciliter.

Embryological Development of the Pancreas[9]

The pancreas is produced in two sections, a dorsal and a ventral. The previous emerges as a diverticulum from the dorsal half of the duodenum a brief separation on top of the hepatic diverticulum, and, changing in to upward and backward into the dorsal mesogastrium, frames a chunk of the head and uncinate method and therefore the entire of the body and tail of the exocrine gland. The ventral part shows up as a diverticulum from the crude bile duct and structures the rest of the head and uncinate procedure of the pancreas.

The duct of the dorsal element during this in this way opens autonomously into the duodenum, whereas that of the ventral part opens with the common bile duct[7].

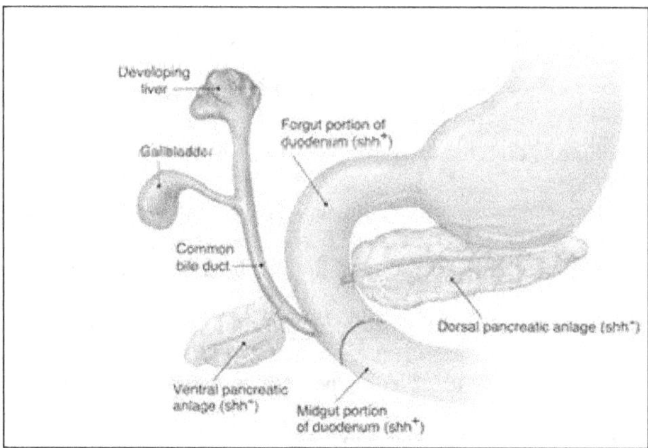

Figure. 1: Development of pancreas

Position and Location of the Pancreas[9]

The pancreas lie more or less transversally over the posterior abdominal wall, at the level of vertebrae Lumbar -1 & Lumbar -2. It is 15 to 20 cm long; about 3 cm broad; and about 2 cm thick. It weighs about 90 g.

ANATOMY OF THE PANCREAS[8]

It is long and sporadically prismatic in shape; its right extremity, being wide, is known as head, and is associated with the fundamental segment of the organ, or body, by a slight tightening, the neck; while its left extremity gradually tapers to form the tail.

Head

The caput pancreatic (head) is smoothed from before in reverse, and is lodged inside the curve of the duodenum. Its upper border is roofed by the superior a part of the duodenum and its lower covers the overlap ahead, and imply themselves behind, the drizzling and ascending parts of the duodenum separately.[7]

Body

The Body of the exocrine gland is elongated. It extends from its neck to the end (tail). It has 3 surfaces: anterior, inferior and posterior. The anterior surface is dish shaped and is directed forwards and upwards. It's lined by peritoneum and is related to the lesser sac and to the stomach. The posterior surface is devoid of peritoneum, and is expounded to: left crus of the diaphragm; the left suprarenal gland, left renal vessels, the aorta with the origin of the superior mesenteric artery and splenic vein. The inferior surface is roofed by peritoneum, associated with duodenojejunal flexure, coils of jejunum, left colic flexure.[7]

Tail

This is the thin left end of the pancreas. It present in the lienorenal ligament commonly with the splenic vessels. It comes in to contact with the lower component of the gastric surface of the spleen.

UNCINATE PROCESS

The angle of intersection of the lower and left lateral borders frames a prolongation, named the uncinate process. It is drained by embellishment pancreatic duct.

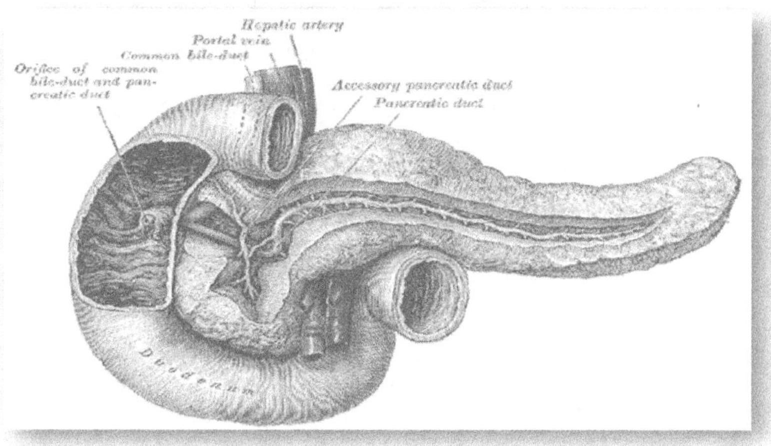

Figure .2: Parts and relations of pancreas

The arterial supply to the pancreas incorporates the; gastroduodenal artery from the common hepatic artery (a branch of celiac trunk); anterior superior pancreaticoduodenal artery from the gastrodudenal artery; posterior superior pancreaticodudenal artery from the gastroduodenal artery ; dorsal pancreatic artery from the inferior pancreatic artery (a branch of the spleenic artery); dorsal pancreatic & greater pancreatic arteries (branches of the spleenic artery); anterior inferior pancreaticoduodenal artery from the inferior pancreaticoduodenal artery (a branch of the superior mesenteric artery); and posterior inferior pancreaticoduodenal artery from the inferior pancreaticoduodenal artery (a branch of the superior mesenteric artery).[9]

DUCTAL SYSTEM OF PANCREAS

The pancreatic duct or ductus pancreaticus stretches out transversely from left to right via the substance of the pancreas. It starts by the intersection of the small ducts of the lobules located in the tail of the pancreas, and, goes from left to right via the body, it gets the ducts of the diverse lobules creating the gland. It achieves the neck where it comes into connection with the common bile duct that lies to its right aspect. Leaving the head of the organ, it goes sideways through the secretion (mucous) and strong layers of the duodenum, and closures by a hole common to it and the common bile duct/channel upon the summit of the major duodenal papilla.[8]

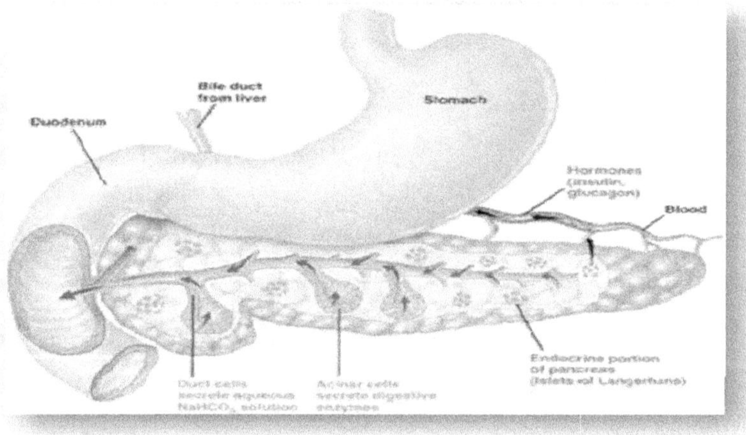

Figure. 3 Ductal System of pancreas.

Accessory pancreatic duct is emitted from the pancreatic duct with in the neck of the pancreas and opens into the duodenum about 2.5 centimeters; over the duodenal papilla on minor duodenal papilla. It gets the conduits from the lower some portion of the head and even the uncinate procedure.

HISTOLOGY OF PANCREAS[9]

In structure, the pancreas takes after the salivary glands. It varies from them, however, in specific points of interest and is looser and milder in its texture. It is n't encased in a distinct capsule, but is surrounded by areolar tissue, which dips in to its inside and interfaces together the various lobules of which it is created. Each lobule look like the lobules of the salivary glands, comprises of one of the definitive ramifications of the main.

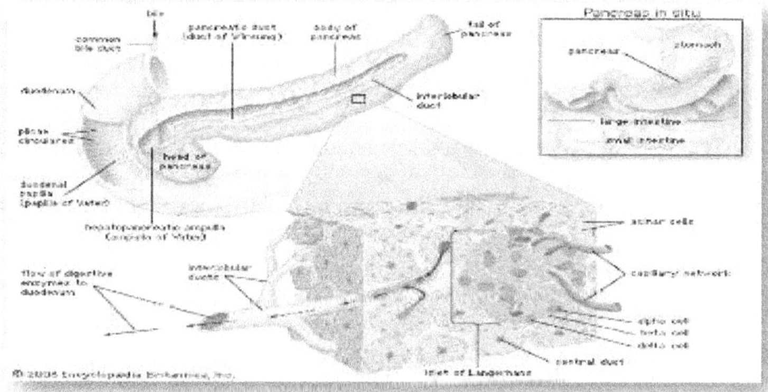

Figure. 4: Histology of the pancreatic islet cell

Duct, finishing in a various of ceacal pouches or alveoli, the alveoli are totally loaded up with secreting cells, the connective tissue between the alveoli presents in certain parts collections of cells, which are named interalveolar cell islands of Langerhans; and are less or more polyhedral in appearance, occur a net work in which ramifies numerous capillaries. There are two main types of cell in the islets, distinguish cells and agreeing β to the special staining reactions of the granules they contain. The cell islets have been delivered the inward emission of the pancreas which is necessary for carbohydrate metabolism. The walls of the pancreatic duct are thin, comprising of two coats, an outer fibrous and an inner mucous.

REGIONAL ANATOMY OF THE ISLET CELLS[9]

Even though islet cells of langerhans were recognized in 1809 as dense clusters of clear cells embedded in the exocrine pancreas, it took nearly 20 years to establish their endocrine function. The major cell varieties of the islet cell cluster are alpha beta delta and gamma cells respectively their major endocrine contribution are glucagon, insulin, stomatostatin, and pancreatic polypeptide respectively. Other products of islets are pancreastatin, chromostatin, islet amyloid polypeptide.

Normal adult pancreas contains 1 million islets. Each islet contains varying number of cells from a dozen to thousand cells. They are thickly situated in the tail of the pancreas. Even though islets occupy only 2-3 % of total pancreatic mass they receive around 20 % of the total pancreatic blood flow and also these areas are richly innervated by coeliac plexus (parasympathetic cholinergic fibers) sympathetic adrenergic fibers.

PHYSIOLOGY OF INSULIN[6]

Insulin was first disengaged from pancreas in 1922 by Banting and Best this almost overnight changed the view point of the severely diabetic patients from one of fast decrease and death to a nearly normal person. Generally insulin has been related with blood sugar and it's true enough that insulin has profound effects on carbohydrate metabolism and also impacts on fat metabolism delivering indirect effects resulting in conditions such as acidosis and arteriosclerosis.

When insulin is secreted:

Insulin is secreted when there is energy abundance i.e. when there is abundance of energy giving foods in the diet especially when there is excess of carbohydrates. Insulin helps in storing up these excess energies. Example is that it removes excess glucose from circulation and stores it in the form of glucagons in liver and muscles.

Insulin chemistry and synthesis[10]

Insulin is a little protein with a relative molecular weight of 5808; it is composed of 2 amino acid chains connected to every alternative with disulfide linkages. Insulin is synthesized in-cells β of islets of langerhans in pancreas. The journey starts as insulin RNA, Insulin prepohormone, and proinsulin and finally insulin is formed. This is secreted in to the blood circulation and in the blood circulation it has a half life about 6 minutes so it is cleared form circulation within a span of 10-15 min. Except for the portion of hypoglycemic agent (insulin) which is in together with receptors within the target cells is degraded by the catalyst insulinase.

Insulin on target cells[6]

Insulin as enzyme acts on the receptors preset on the target cells and thus elaborates the functions. When insulin binds with the receptors β-subunits that area unit protruding into the cytomembrane gets phosphorylated. This autophosphosrylation of other intracellular enzymes called insulin receptor substrates they activate a particular enzyme and inactive others [according to the target tissue] thus controlling intracellular metabolic machinery producing desired impacts on fat, protein and carbohydrate metabolism.

Effects of insulin on carbohydrate metabolism[11]

Immediately after a high carbohydrate meal lot of glucose appears in blood circulation this triggers secretion of insulin. This causes rapid uptake of glucose into the cells and is stored up for further utility. During much part of the day the muscle tissue depends on the fatty acids for its energy the reason for this being, the membrane of the muscle is only permeable to fatty acids.

So it depends on fatty acids but when there is presence of insulin especially after a meal increases the permeability for glucose and thus uptake of glucose also increases.

Effects of insulin on fat metabolism[12]

Because the future effects of insulin lack end up in atherosclerosis frequently prompting to heart attacks, cerebral stroke, and different vascular accidents. Insulin helps in glucose uptake by the cells of the body and thus acts as a fat sparer.

Insulin increases glucose uptake by liver cells, excess formation of citrate and isocitrate which are precursors of fatty acid synthesis.

Effects of insulin on protein metabolism

Insulin has the effect even putting the proteins to a storage form and stimulates transport of many amino acids in to the cell. It also increases the translation of messenger RNA, and the rate of transcription of the selected DNA. Insulin inhibits the amino acid catabolism and thus favors release of amino acids from the cells, decreases the process of gluconeogenesis in the liver thus sparing the proteins.[13]

Control of insulin secretion[10]

It is formerly believed that insulin is the only factor that regulates the blood glucose levels in the body. Now we know about other regulating factors because of insulin action on fatty acids and amino acids.

Table.1 Factors and conditions that regulate the insulin secretion[6]

Increased insulin secretion	Decreased insulin secretion
Increased blood glucose	Decreased Blood Glucose
Increased serum free fatty acids	Fasting
Increased serum amino acids	Somatostatin
Gastrointestinal hormone	Alpha Adrenergic Activity
[gastrin, secretin, cholecystokinin]	Leptin
Glucagons, growth hormone, cortisone.	
Parasympathetic stimulation [acetylcholine]	
Beta adrenergic stimulation.	
Insulin resistance obesity.	
Sulfonylurea drugs [glyburide, tolbutamide]	

Increased blood glucose[6]

Normal fasting blood glucose level is 80-90mg/100ml. To this level insulin secretion rate is 25 ng/min/kg body weights. When Plasma glucose concentration increases by 3 times the normal then Plasma insulin secretion increases almost 10 folds in 3-5min. (this is just immediate dumping of preformed insulin from the beta cells of islets of langerhans). Within 5-10 min insulin levels falls down to normal. After 15min again for the 2nd time there will be raise in insulin level and reaches maximum by 2-3hours. (This is a result of release of remaining preformed insulin and newly synthesized insulin from pancreas).

FEEDBACK REGULATION:

Increased blood glucose levels [positive feedback] triggers the insulin secretion. Insulin secretion when raises causes up taking of plasma glucose into the cells thus lowering the plasma glucose concentration [negative feedback]; this in turn reduce the insulin secretion from the pancreas.

OTHER FACTORS:

Amino acids potentiate the sugar/glucose stimulus for insulin secretion i.e. insulin promotes transport of amino acids in to the tissue cells as well as intracellular formation of proteins.

Gastrointestinal hormones:

Gastrin, secretin, cholecystokinin, gastric repressive proteins area unit free in response to a meal. These hormones in turn increase the plasma insulin levels known as anticipatory raised in preparation for the glucose and amino acids to be absorbed from food.

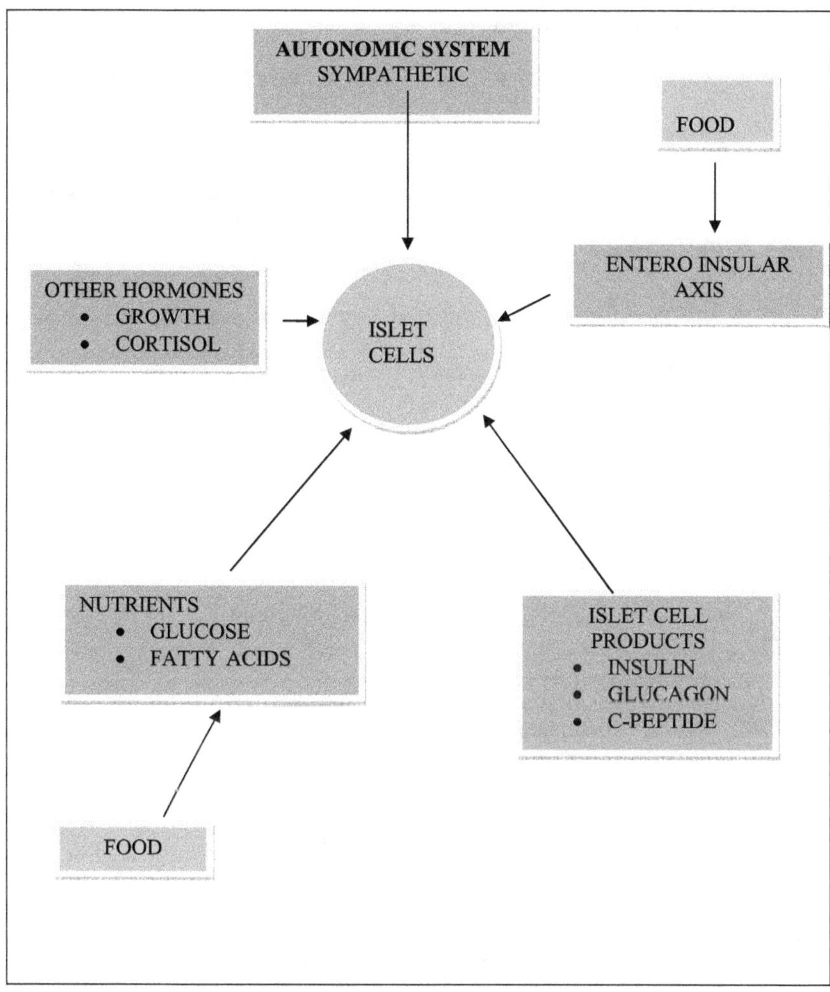

Figure .5 Factors regulating the islet cell secretion[7]

Other hormones:

Hormones like glucagons, growth hormone, cortisol and estrogen and progesterone potentially increases insulin secretion. But long term stimulation of these hormones results in exhaustion of beta cells and increasing risk of diabetes mellitus.

Autonomic nervous system:

Increased parasympathetic stimulation to pancreas may result in increased insulin secretion

UNDERSTANDING THE DIFFERENT COMPONENTS OF THE DISEASE DEFNITION

Diabetes mellitus is a clinical disorder portrayed by hyperglycemia because of outright or relative inadequacy of insulin. There is aggravation of intermediary metabolism mainly manifesting as constant hyperglycemia[11].

Diabetes mellitus is characterized as a disturbance of intermediary metabolism showing as associate continuing hyperglycemia, primarily because of either associate absolute or relative absence of insulin.

There are two widely known forms[13]

- Type I diabetes mellitus
- Type II diabetes mellitus

WHO recognizes three main forms of diabetes mellitus[14]

- Type I diabetes mellitus
- Type II diabetes mellitus
- Gestational diabetes

TYPE I DIABETES MELLITUS [15]
(Failure of pancreas to produce insulin)

In this type there is autoimmune destruction of beta cells resulting in lack of production of insulin and there by resulting in hyperglycemia.

TYPE 2 DIABETES MELLITUS[16]

(Characterized by insulin resistance in target cells)

Production of insulin secretion from the pancreas is completely normal however take up of insulin by receptors in muscle are lacking or meager leading to a condition of relative lack of insulin and there by setting up hyperglycemia.

GESTATIONAL DIABETES

(This type refers to acute worry of pregnancy made by pregnancy related hormones on pancreas)

This again is characterized by insulin resistance in target cells created by the hormones of pregnancy.

ETIOLOGICAL CLASSIFICATION[17]

Type 1 Diabetes

Islet beta cell destruction usually resulting in absolute insulin deficiency

- Immune mediated

- Idiopathic

Type 2 Diabetes

Heterogeneous – starting from preponderantly insulin resistance with relative insulin deficiency to preponderantly insulin deficiency with insulin resistance.

OTHER SPECIFIC TYPES[18]

- Genetic defects of cell functione .g. MODY syndrome.
- Genetic defects in insulin action e.g. Leprechaunism.
- Diseases of the exocrine pancreas e.g. Pancerarititis.
- Secondary to endocrinopathies e.g. Acromegaly.

- Drugs or chemical induced e.g. glucocorticoids.

- Infections e.g. Congenital rubella Cytomegalo virus others.

- Uncommon forms of IMD (immune mediated diabetes) e.g. Anti insulin receptor antibodies and others etc.,

- Genetic syndromes associated with diabetes e.g. Down's syndrome.

GESTATIONAL DIABETES MELLITUS[19]

Diabetes or impaired tolerance diagnosed in pregnancy – includes pre existing diabetes.

TYPE 2 DIABETES[16]

The primary problem is decreased sensitivity of the target tissues (mostly affecting the cells of muscle and fat tissues) to the metabolic effects of the insulin, termed as "insulin resistance". There also is a process of increase blood glucose.

Initially production of insulin is to beat the amount of resistance. But gradually production declines and insulin cannot be discharged as vigorously resulting in hyperglycemia. There are basically two groups of factors controlling this phenomenon of disease evolution they are genetic factors and environmental risk factors[4].

Genetic factors[20]

Genetic factors are more important in the etiology of type 2 diabetes than type 1 as shown by the studies in monozygotic twins where concordance rate approach 100 %. Type 2 diabetes has complex or polygenic pattern of inheritance, which suggests it's related to the results of the multiple genes together with lifestyle and environmental factors. Thus believed to bring a strong genetic link, and thus it tends to run in families.

Risk factors[21]

- Obesity (especially apple type).

- Family history of type 2 diabetes mellitus.

- Age above 40 years.

- Sedentary lifestyle.

- History of gestational diabetes or birth of large babies.

- Past impaired glucose tolerance.

- Westernized diet habits like red meat high fats and more sugar etc.,

- Ethnicity is more common in non Hispanics of northern European descent.

- Cigarette smoking decreases insulin sensitivity.

- Malnutrition in utero.

The relation between growing age and the interaction between the genetic and the environmental factors in the evolution of type 2 diabetes mellitus can be better visualized in the following picture.

The most important of the environment risk factors are obesity, physical inactivity, repeated pregnancies, infection, physical or psychological stress and diabetogenic drugs.

This type of diabetes is also called as maturity onset diabetes mellitus it comprises of about 85-90% of all diabetics. The evolution of the pathophysiology of this type of diabetes is complex and two important factors that work in tandem for the evolution and progress of the disorder are

- Insulin resistance

- Relative insulin deficiency

Insulin resistance

Insulin resistance refers to decreased sensitivity of the peripheral receptors to the insulin resulting in

- Decreased uptake of glucose in to the cells.
- Raised plasma glucose concentration
- Suppression of hepatic glucose production
- Lipolysis in response to insulin.

The seats of insulin resistance are considered as muscles liver and adipose tissue[22].

Relative insulin deficiency

Actually there is no direct decrease in the secretion of the insulin as researched in type 2 diabetes in contrast with type 1.

Genetic and environmental factors –cell contribute loss from the pancreatic to the Islets.

Early in the illness procedure there is hyperplasia of-cells resulting the pancreas in misrepresented insulin and proinsulin reactions to glucose (hyper insulinism).

In chronicity there is deposition of amyloid in the islets as there is associated genetically inherited defect there is inability of the system to clear these deposits ultimately resulting in progressive impairment cell function and decreased of the β secretion.

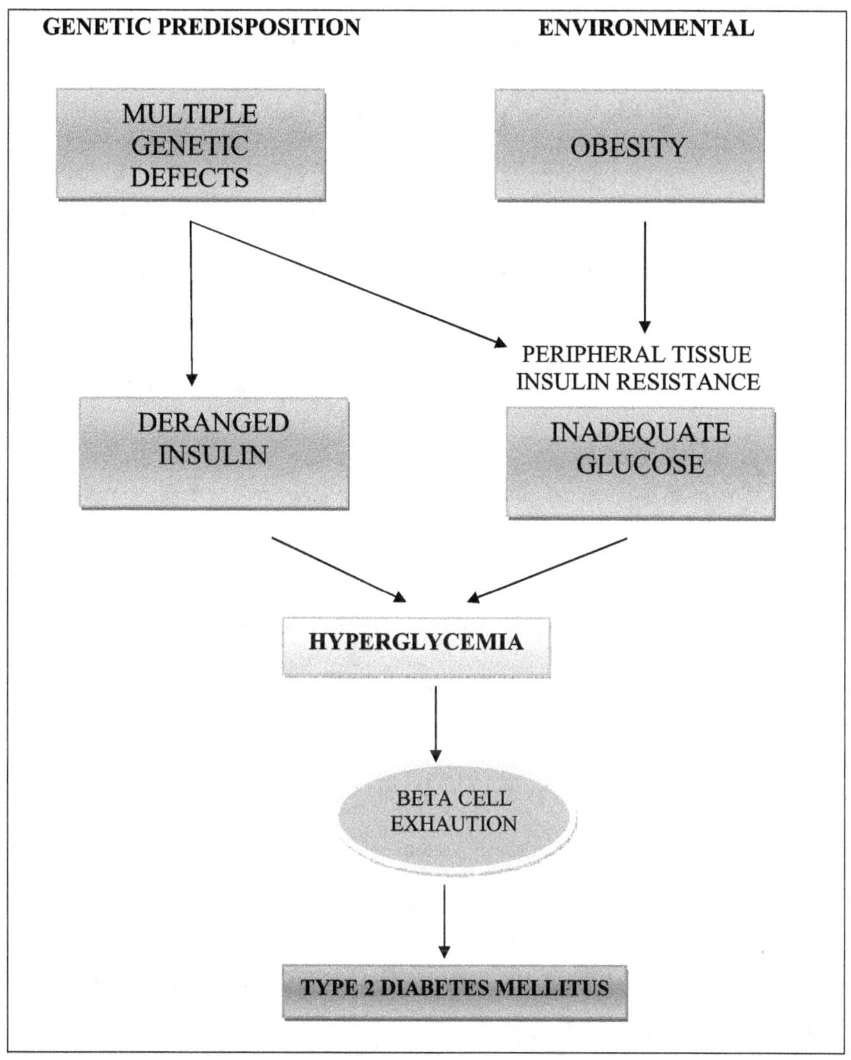

Figure. 6 Pathophysiology of type 2 diabetes mellitus[23]

We generally observe that type 2 diabetes is more serious and complicated in obese individuals because of the following reasons.

OBESITY, INSULIN RESISTANCE AND DIABETES[22]

Obesity is linked with type 2 diabetes, although not with type 1, because it results in insulin resistance. About eighty percentages of those with type 2 diabetes are obesity and therefore the risk of developing the disease will be increases progressively, when the body mass index, waist to hip quantitative relation, waist circumference, or, a lot of specifically, the number of deep abdominal body fat will increases. Although body mass index has been the most commonly cited risk factor for developing diabetes, research shows that waist circumference of more than 88cms in women and 102cms in men is a highest risk of developing type 2 diabetes and cardiovascular complications.

Changes in the number, type and location of the fat cells in the body fat, muscles and liver are central to the development of insulin resistance in obese people. Large, insulin resistant fat cells in deep abdominal fat release increased amounts of non esterified fatty acids in to the portal vein, from where they enter the liver and then the general circulation.

Non esterified (free) fatty acids increase hepatic glucose and triglyceride output in to the circulation (leading to hyperglycemia and dyslipidemia). They also inhibit uptake of glucose by skeletal muscle (causing insulin resistance) and release- of I cells further worsening glucose production by the liver. High levels of glucose and lipids are also directly toxic to β-cells, reducing insulin secretion. Other substances released by fat cells, such as TNF and IL -6, also worsen insulin resistance. The protein adiponectin counteracts insulin resistance, but people with abdominal obesity have lower circulating levels of these proteins. Fat cells also secrete angiotensin II, which raises blood pressure and promotes atherosclerosis.

NEFA also directly injures the endothelial cells coating the blood vessels, further worsening such changes. Thus it is evident how excess deep abdominal fat may lead to insulin obstruction, type 2 diabetes, abnormal blood fat levels, and increased cardiovascular risks.

Visceral fat correlates with insulin resistance but whereas subcutaneous fat is not responsible with respect to insulin resistance. Best example is Japanese sumo wrestlers whose extreme obesity is predominantly sub cutaneous. Their daily vigorous exercise programmers prevent accumulation of the visceral fat and thus have normal serum lipids and hyperglycemia despite daily intake of 5000-7000 k cal.

PATHOPHYSIOLOGY[23]

Whatever may be the type of diabetes either it is type 1 or type 2 there will be lack of insulin absolutely or relatively. This lack of insulin brings about 2 necessary changes specifically/namely –

- ↓ (decreased) anabolism.
- ↑ (increased) catabolism.

These damaging changes can be prevented, or at least moderated; through diet and exercise particularly at the stage of prediabetes reducing the risk of developing diabetes and this has been demonstrated by several large clinical studies. Exercise is particularly effective in reducing deep body fat cell mass.

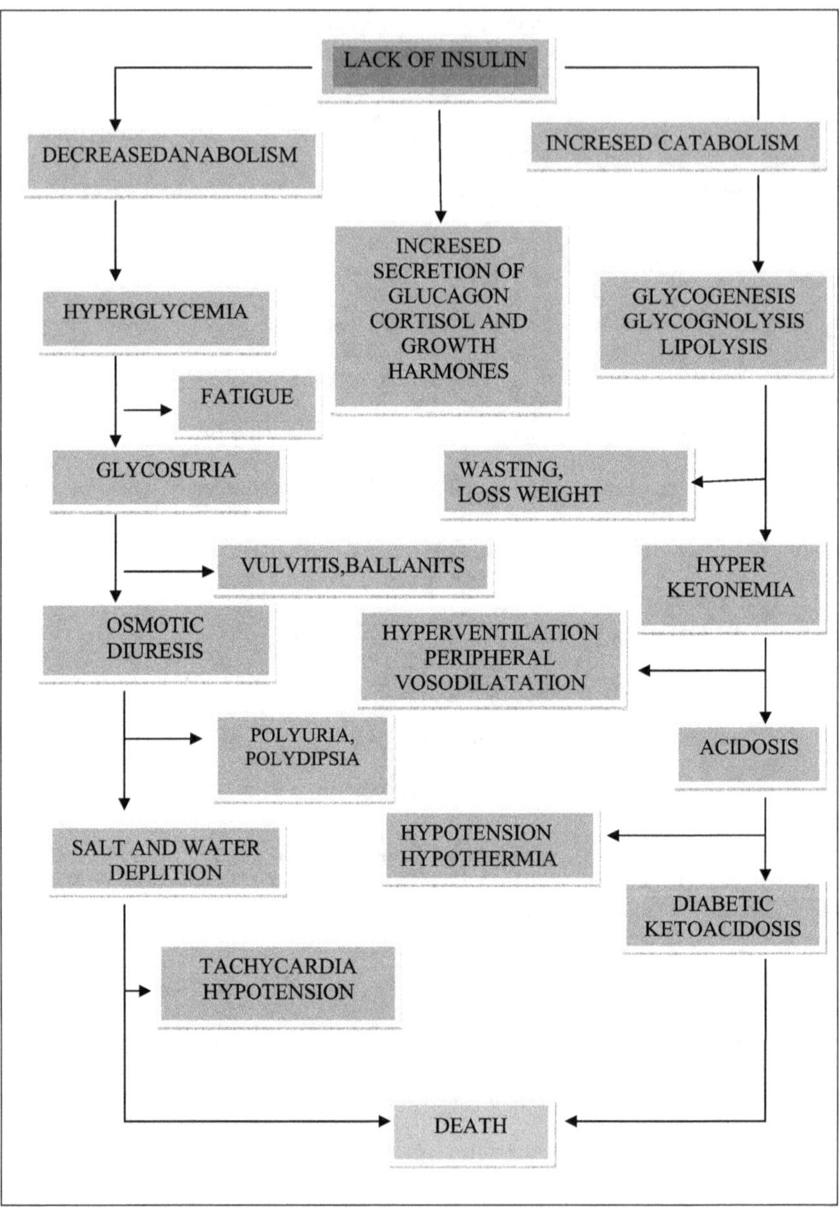

Figure .7 Overall changes of diabetes in a simple flow chart form [25]

CLINICAL PRESENTATION[24]

Hyperglycemia presents with a wide range of symptoms out of them classical features are as follows.

- Polyuria

- Polydipsia

- Increased frequency of urination in night times

- Quick tiredness

- Loss of weight

- Loss of sharpness of eye sight

- Sensitiveness of Pruritus

- Genital infections.

- Recurrent headache along with nausea.

- Excessive appetite.

- $\uparrow$ Predilection to sugar items.

- Mood swings and agitation.

- Cannot concentration on work.

- Frequent urinary tract infections.

- Slow healing of wounds.

- Dry or pruritic skin.

INVESTIGATIONS

Blood Sugar Testing[26]

Blood sugar concentration, or sugar level, refers to the live of glucose present in the blood of a person's or creature. Ordinarily, in mammals the blood glucose level is kept up at a reference go between about 3.6 and 5.8mmol/l. It is firmly regulated as a part of metabolic homeostasis.

There are different modes of estimating the levels of blood sugar levels.

Table. 2 Fasting Blood Glucose Levels

Fasting Blood Glucose	
GLUCOSE LEVEL	**INDICATION**
From 70 to 99 mg/dL (3.9 to 5.5 mmol/L)	Normal fasting glucose
From 100 to 125 mg/dL (5.6 to 6.9 mmol/L)	Impaired fasting glucose (pre – diabetes)
126 mg/dL (7.0 mmol/L) and above on more than one testing occasion.	Diabetes

Random Blood Glucose Levels [27]

Random blood sugar test gives your blood glucose during a day. Normal random blood glucose level should be < (less than) 200mg/dl.

If your random blood sugar/glucose level is between 140mg/dl to 200mg/dl, then may have pre diabetes.

100-140mg/dl can be considered as a normal range.

Table. 3 Oral Glucose Tolerance Test[28] (other than pregnant womens)

Oral Glucose Tolerance Test (OGTT)

Levels applicable except during pregnancy. Sample drawn 2 hours after a 75-gram glucose drink.

GLUCOSE LEVEL	INDICATION
Less than 140 mg/dL (7.8 mmol/L)	Normal glucose tolerance
From 140 to 200 mg/dL (7.8 to 11.1 mmol/L)	Impaired glucose tolerance (pre-diabetes)
Over 200 mg/dL (11.1 mmol/L) on more than one testing occasion	Diabetes

Table. 4 Oral Glucose Challenge Test

Gestational Diabetes Screening: Glucose Challenge Test

Sample drawn 1 hour after a 50-gram glucose drink.

GLUCOSE LEVEL	INDICATION
Less than 140* mg/dL (7.8 mmol/L)	Normal screen
140* mg/dL (7.8 mmol/L) and over	Abnormal, needs OGTT (see below)

* Some use a cutoff of >130 mg/dL (7.2 mmol/L) because that identifies 90% of women with gestational diabetes, compared to 80% identified using the threshold of >140 mg/dL (7.8 mmol/L).

Table . 5 Oral Glucose tolerance test (exclusively pregnancy oriented)

Gestational Diabetes Diagnostic : OGTT	
Sample drawn after 100 gram glucose drink	
TIME OF SAMPLE COLLECTION	TARGET LEVELS
Fasting*(prior to glucose load)	95 mg/dL(5.3 mmol/L)
1 hour after glucose load	180 mg/dL(10.0 mmol/L)
2 hours after glucose load	155 mg/dL(8.6 mmol/L)
3 hour after glucose load*	140 mg/dL(7.8 mmol/L)
INDICATION: If two or more values meet or exceed the diabetes is diagnosed.	target levels, gestational

Glycosylated Hemoglobin

Glycosylated hemoglobin (Hba1c) could be a form of hemoglobin utilized primarily to identify the normal plasma sugar fixation over prolonged periods of time. It is framed in a non enzymatic pathway by hemoglobin's ordinary presentation to high plasma levels of glucose. Normal range is 4.0- 5.9 %.

URINE TESTING

Glucose

Testing the urine for glucose is the usual technique for recognizing diabetes. If possible testing should be performed on the urine passed 1-2 hours after food, since this will distinguish more number of diabetes than fasting specimen. The best disadvantage of using urinary glucose as a diagnostic method is the individual variety in renal threshold for glucose, which is basic during pregnancy and youngsters.

Ketones

Ketonuria can also be present during fasting, strenuous exercise for long periods, severe vomiting or due to diet high in fats and low in carbohydrates. Ketonuria, thus not pathognomonic of diabetes, however once related to glycosuria, the diagnosis of diabetes is very possible.

Protein

Urine testing for albumin is a standard testing procedure to identify the presence of renal disease or UTI in people with diabetes.

Testing for sugar using dipsticks there's a greatest disadvantage is that individual variation in renal threshold for sugar. For ketone bodies using nitroprusside response, this is often primarily specific for acetoacetate conventionally administered out using tablets, dipsticks for finding proteins. Presence of proteins indicates some renal pathology secondary to diabetes.

COMPLICATIONS[29]

Acute complications

- Chronic renal failure(nephropathy)[30]

- Hypoglycemia

- Ketoacidosis or non ketotic hyperosmolar coma

- Chronic complication

- Cardiovascular disease[31]

- Retinal damage(retinopathy)[32]

- Nerve damage(neuropathy)[33]

- Micro vascular damage (microangiopathy)

And these complications may still progress to

- Impotence

- Poor healing

- Gangrene

- Sometimes may require amputation

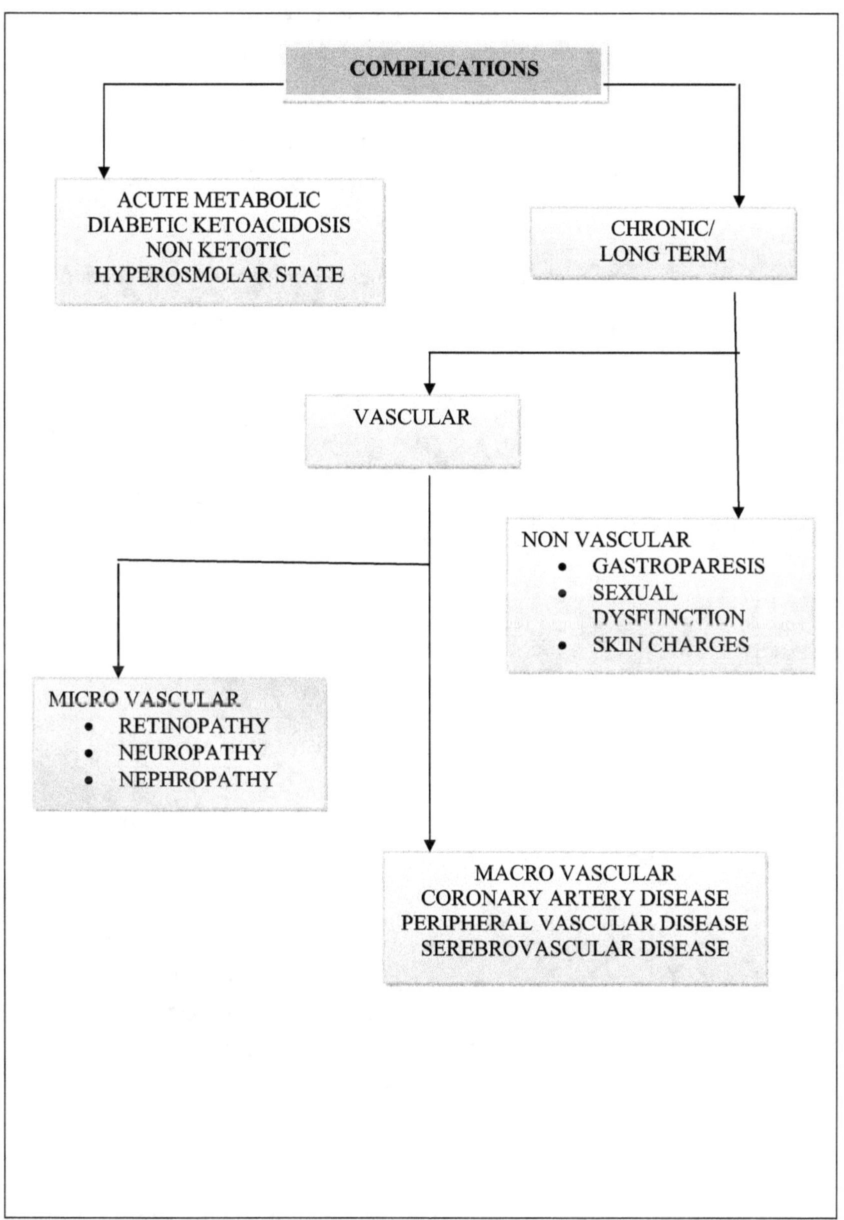

Figure. 8 Complications of diabetes mellitus in flow chart form[29]

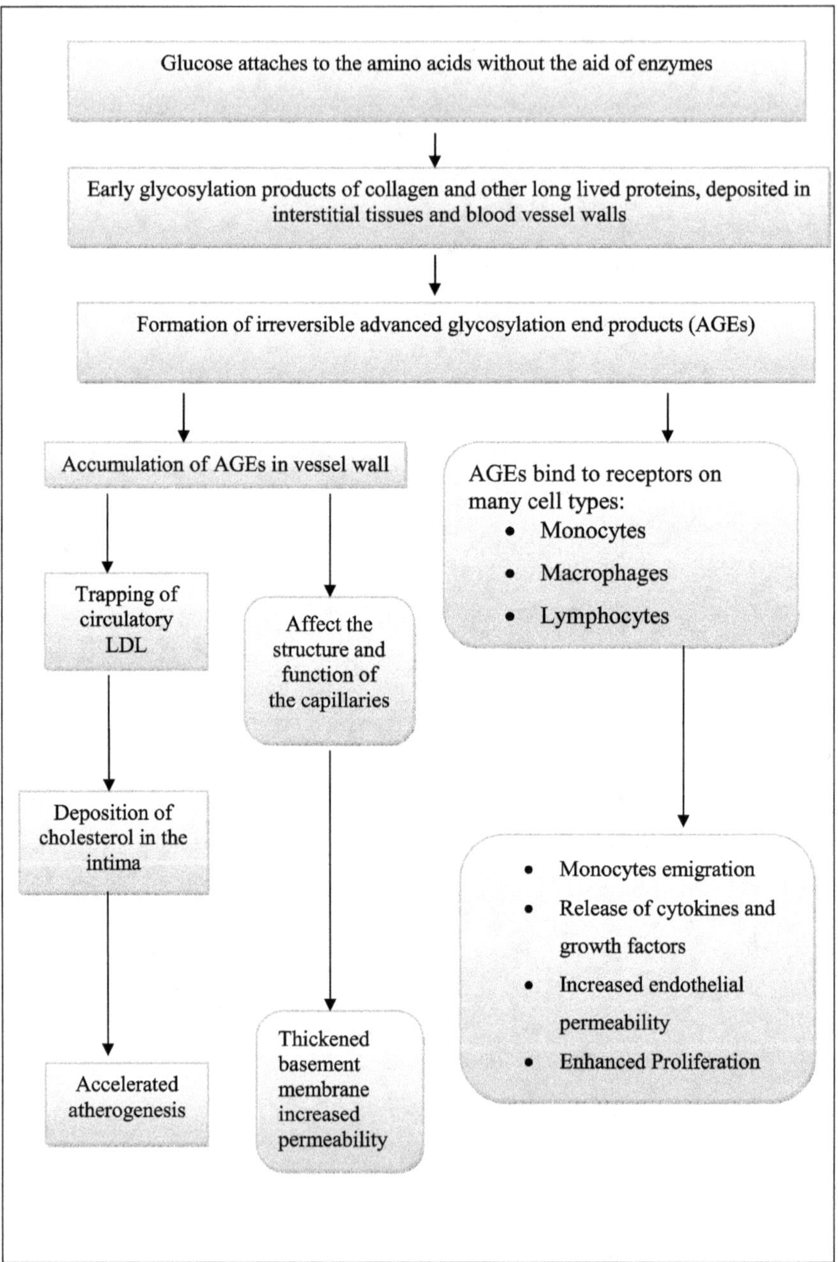

Figure . 9 Root pathogenetic mechanisms that result in complications of diabetes mellitus[23]

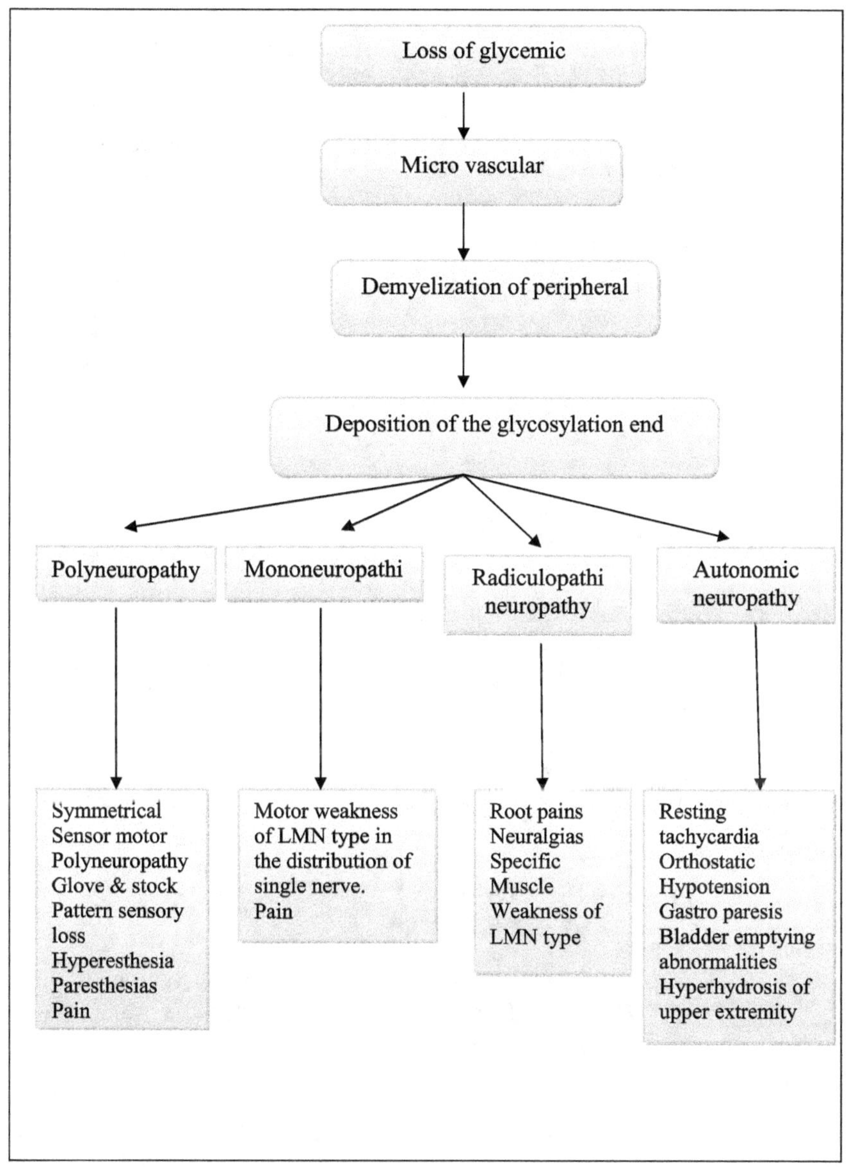

Figure. 10 Pathogenesis of neuropathy in diabetes mellitus[33]

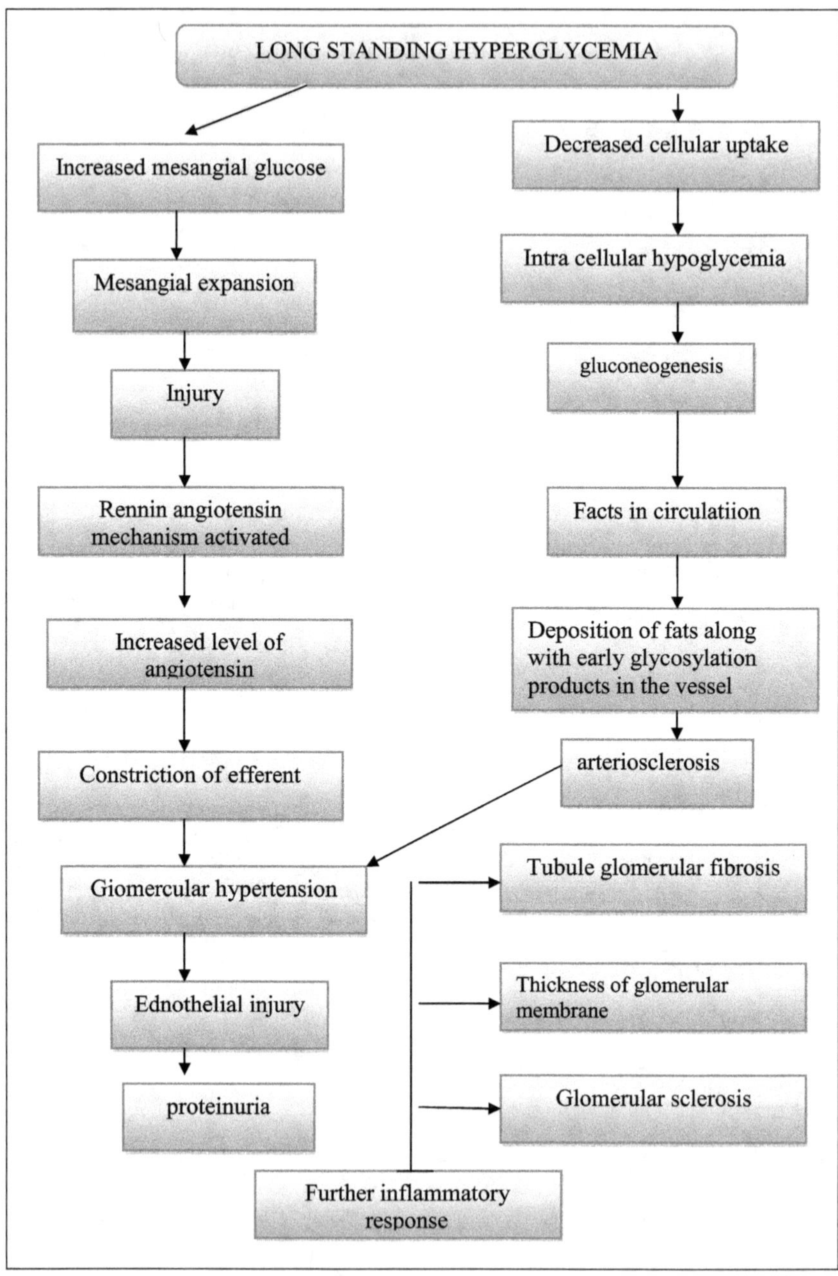

Figure .11 Pathogenesis of nephropathy in diabetes mellitus[30]

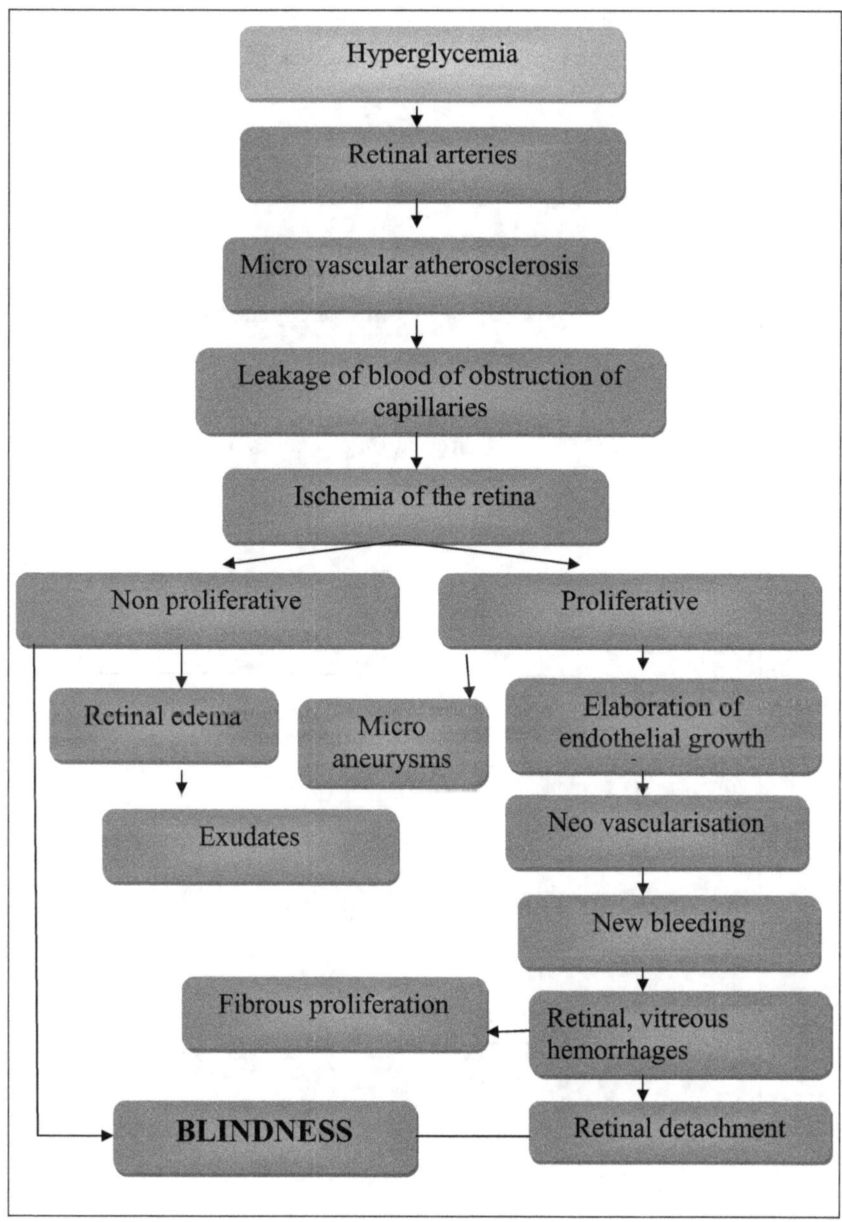

Figure .12: Pathogenesis of retinopathy in diabetes mellitus[32]

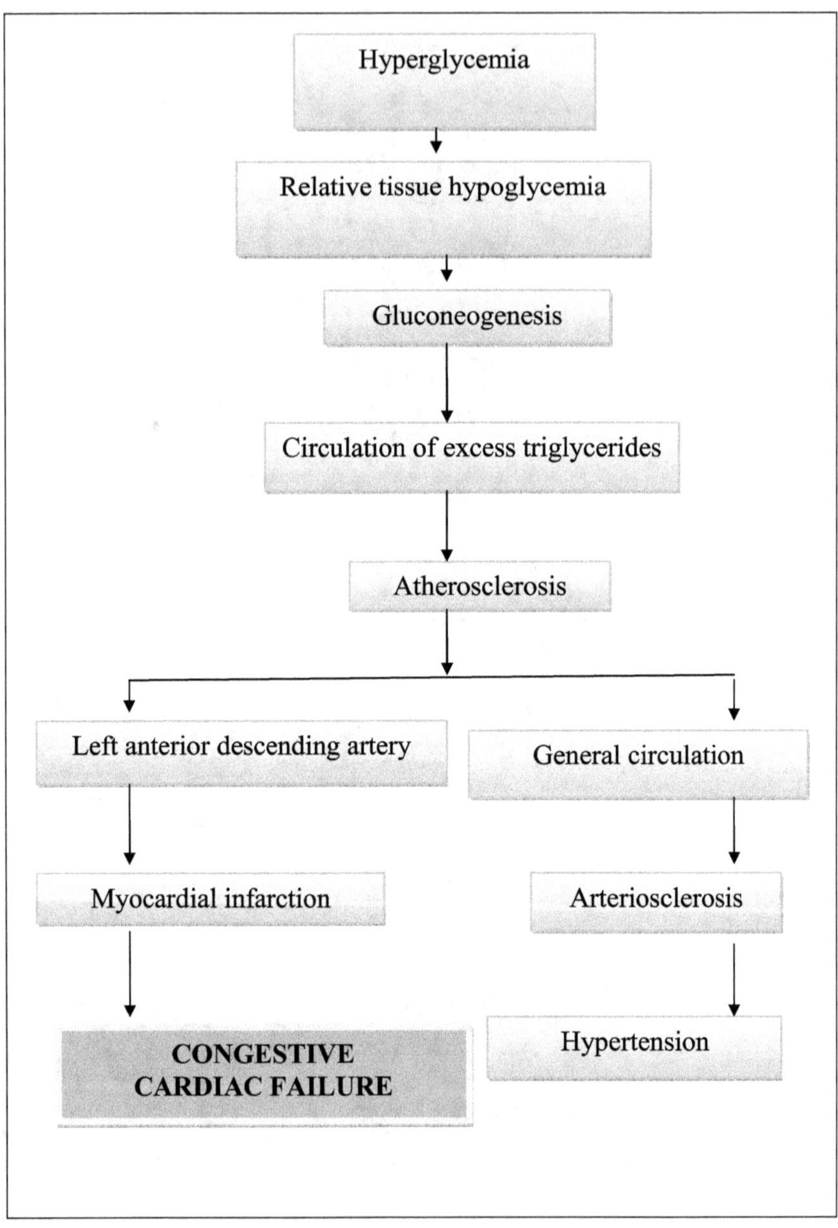

Figure .13: Pathogenesis of cardiac morbidity in diabetes mellitus[31]

Major complications of the type 2 diabetes mellitus are nephropathy, neuropathy retinopathy and cardiac morbidity. Diabetic ketoacidosis and hyperosmolar non ketotic coma are the two acute complications in case of type 1 diabetes but their possibility cannot be ruled out in case of type 2 diabetes also.

Other complications like infections in general which comes up as a result of the hyperglycemic state

INFECTIONS:

It causes considerable mortality and morbidity in patients with diabetes. Infections may encourage metabolic disturbances and conversely the metabolic confusions can be the cause of the further infections.

The examples of such infections are malignant otitis media, rhinocerebral mucormycosis, and emphysematous pyelonephritis; occur almost in patient with diabetes. Infections like staphylococcal sepsis occur more frequently and can result in death of the patient. Hyperglycemia and acidemia worsen debilitations in body substance immunity and polymorphonuclear leucocyte and white corpuscle works but are considerably, if not completely reversed once P_H and the blood sugar levels are come to normal range.

Osteomyelitis persistent spread of a polymicrobial contamination from a skin ulcer to adjacent bone is regular in patients with diabetes resulting in osteomyelitis.

Other complications like gastroparesis which results in mild APD symptoms and also constipation it is mostly related to autonomic neuropathic changes of diabetes mellitus. The next one to be discussed is the sexual dysfunction it is again a common associative of diabetic adults this can be a part of autonomic and radiculopathic complication and also a sequel of metabolic syndrome[34].

MANAGEMENT OF TYPE 2 DIABETES MELLITUS[35]

Maintenance of the blood glucose levels is essential to feel healthy and avoiding long term complications of diabetes. Some people are able to control their glucose levels with diet and exercise alone where as others may require insulin or other medications in addition to life style changes. In other terms management is a lifelong affair and patient need to be oriented regarding this.

OBJECTIVES OF MANAGEMENT

Maintenance of the blood glucose levels is essential to feel healthy and avoiding long term complications of diabetes. Some people are able to control their sugar levels with diet and exercise alone where as others may require insulin or other medications in addition to life style changes. In other terms management is a lifelong affair and patient need to be oriented regarding this.

Management is broadly divided in to general and specific where specific has to directly counter the blood glucose levels or the pancreatic cells. While general management offers a general approach to our body improving the vitality to withstand and eradicate diabetes.

The main areas of concentration needed in managing diabetes mellitus type 2 through general management are -

- Regular monitoring of blood sugar levels
- Diet control and a healthy diet
- Exercise guidelines
- Integrated approach in treating diabetes.

MONITORING THE BLOOD GLUCOSE LEVELS[36]

As the amount of blood glucose levels are ever fluctuating, self monitoring makes one cognizant to what makes blood sugar levels rise and fall, so that adjustments could be made accordingly.

The best range for patients depends on have complications of diabetes, a typical target range might be 80-120 mg/dl and below 180mg/dl for postprandial reference. In case of older individuals who have complications from their disease may have a fasting target goal of 100-140mg/dl and less than 200mg/dl for postprandial reference. If the patient is on insulin then blood sugar monitored at least twice a day. Glycated hemoglobin or HbA1C is also used for monitoring the patients in the treatment of diabetes mellitus[26].

DIET CONTROL AND A HEALTHY DIET[27]

Patients with diabetes mellitus type 2 are kept on a1500-1800 calorie diet per day in order to promote weight reduction and then to maintain a perfect body weight. More obese people may need more calories at initially until their weight is decrease. This is because it takes more calories to keep up a larger body and a 1600 calorie diet for them may advance weight reduction that is too fast to be healthy.

However diet plan may depend on person's.

- Age
- Sex
- Activity level
- Current weight
- Body weight

Diet plays a significant role in controlling diabetes. Fundamental objective of the diabetic diet is to maintain a perfect body weight and to prevent overabundance weight gain. The diet plan for diabetic patient is depends on weight, age, height, sex, physical movement and nature of diabetes. While getting ready for diet complications such as hypertension, elevated cholesterol levels must be considered[38].

The arrangement includes the type of food to be taken, amount of food to be taken, and also at what time it can be consumed should be given such factors.

Carbohydrates[11]

It should give 55% to 60% of add up to body calories, most complex carbohydrates like vegetables, fruits, beans, whole grains, cereals presents low glycemic index.

Fats[12]

It should provide 25-35% of total body calories polyunsaturated fatty acids and monounsaturated fatty acids helps increase the HDL cholesterol and decrease the LDL cholesterol. And these fatty acids are available in olives, peanuts, canola oils, avocados, nuts and omega 3 polyunsaturated fatty acids in fish, flax seeds, walnuts. And saturated fats like red meat and butter to less than 7% of daily calories. Limit trans fat (hydrogenated fat) which is found in snack foods, fried food to not exactly 1% of total calories.

Proteins[13]

It should give 12-20% of add up to body calories, although this may vary depending on the patients individual health requirements. Patients with kidney disease should confine protein to under 10% of calories, soy, fish and poultry are the preferred choices than red meat.

Fiber

It should be 20-35 grams per day. Reduce salt intake, less salt should be used in cooking, food could be flavored with herbs and spices.

The diabetic diet can be divided under a food pyramid then the order of the food in the pyramids is arranged in six groups in ascending order they are

- Grains and Starches

- Vegetables

- Fruits

- Milk

- Meat and meat substitutes

- Fats sweets and alcohol

A sample diet schedule is constructed on the basis of above given standard instructions and patients are thoroughly explained regarding what to eat, when to eat, how much to eat a time. Then patient are followed up regarding their diet [39] regularities according to the chart prescribed to them.

EXERCISE AND DIABETES [40]

Exercises will possibly management the diabetes by non medical means and also to decrease the complication of the disease, considerably less the risk of chronic complications. Exercise helps control –

- Bodyweight

- Blood glucose levels

Thus lowers risk of heart diseases Exercise makes one feel better about themselves and increase their overall health.

Type of exercise required depends on the health status of the person i.e. whether the person is already having any other complaints or health problems. Most of the doctor's advices for aerobics like-

- Walking

- Aerobic, Jogging and bicycling

These aerobic exercises help heart to work harder. When the diabetic state is associated with problems of the feet or legs then the type of exercise required is that without putting much stress on the feet. These exercises include bicycling and swimming etc,

ORAL DRUG THERAPY[41]

If the patients with type 2 diabetes not achieved suitable control after three months of dietary modification and more physical activity, then oral antidiabetic (anti hyperglycemic) may be tried. Two major classes are the sulfonylureas and the biguanides.

Sulfonylureas

It acts primarily by ↑ (increasing) endogenous insulin secretion.

Biguanides

It act chiefly by diminishing hepatic gluconeogenesis and expanding peripheral utililization of glucose. Both types function only in the presence of some endogenous insulin production.

Most patients with type 2 diabetes mellitus are excessive weight, and are preferably manage with the biguanide metformin rather than with a sulfonylurea (which can cause weight gain). In patients who are not obese preferably can be started on with sulfonylureas like chlorpropamide and glybenclamide

Other drugs include alpha glucosidase inhibitor such as acarbose and miglitol. These act by deferring the absorption of the glucose from the gastro intestinal tract. Combined drug therapies like triple therapy which includes metformin, sulfonylurea, and either rosiglitazone or pioglitazone has been shown to be effective.

Insulin Therapy[42]

The aim of insulin treatment is to achieve the best ideal control of blood sugar concentration without the risk of the hypoglycemia. Tight management of blood sugar concentration can diminish the future complications of diabetes like microvascular and macrovascular complications.

The insulin available today is a biotechnology derived product that is pure and causes fewer allergic side effects than the older beef and pork products. While insulin may not be necessary part of management of type 2 diabetes, it is essential in the treatment of type 1, since they have little or no endogenous insulin secretory limit.

Even though type 2 diabetes which cannot be controlled adequately by oral therapy and diet, need insulin either in addition or in place of oral treatment.

The types of insulin used are generally three types, they are-

- o Short acting insulin
- o Long acting insulin
- o Mixed variety

Most normally long acting insulin and mixed variety are used. The dosage of insulin is determined on the grounds of plasma glucose levels, complications, and also general state of the patient. The homoeopathic management of it is detailed in the next heading homoeopathy and diabetes[43].

HOMOEOPATHY AND DIABETES

Diabetes is a disease, the origin and therefore the explanation for that little known and hidden in obscurity, has naturally taxed the energies of medical community altogether ages. Consequently there's a vast array or numerous medicines that are prescribed for this compliant. Historically diabetes been treated with great number of specifics proposed for its treatment and it is not surprising. The cause for this being the irremediable character of the illness. But homoeopathy is accepted for its holistic approach towards diseases

HERBERT A ROBERTS OPINIONS ABOUT DIABETES[44]

The view point of the modern psychologist reflects the theory that the overwhelming majority of human diseases are traceable to dysfunctions of the organ system. He saw that the perform of a number of the ductless glands is to secrete a small quantity of the specialised product within the system a secretion that features a important relating the health of the entire constitutions. In many cases this secretions of an ordinary organs is so minute that it approaches the homoeopathic lessening.

Like homoeopathic remedies these glands also helps in maintaining the health with infinitesimal amounts of the secretions, we can hardly fail to see the important relationship these homoeopathic remedy could hold to the indications of the insulin dysfunction and to the equalization of the ductless glands.

His observation about insulin that once insulin is given patient tends to depend on it and there is little hope of building up normal balance. Consequently it is more reasonable to begin management by using homoeopathic remedies.

SHANKARN'S VIEW ON DIABETES[45]

Vital to developing the homoeopathic vision is the understanding of what is to be cured in the disease. It is to be able to perceive, feel and to know as the truth that disease is not something local but a disturbance of the whole being. It is to own the unwavering conviction that if we treat the illness at the centre the local issues are diminished. Diabetes is one such disease with a middle disturbance presenting with local manifestations. Hence diabetes also requires an approach where the centre or core is to be aimed and this is done by giving constitutional approach to the patient.

HAHNEMANN'S ORGANON OF MEDICINE[46]

Constitutional approach means where the mind, physical make up, general behavior, along with particulars of the disease will be considered in the totality. There is a long running debate about the consideration of mind for prescribing by homoeopaths. And one more important thing is which aspect of the is to be given importance or the whole, for this master Hahnemann has explained in his organon of medicine in aphorism number two hundred eleven which reads,

"This holds great to such an extent, that primary determines the choice of the homoeopathic medicine".

Remedy which covers the psychological state and the general manifestation of the patient has a more possibility of relieving than the one that covers the particulars.

Concept of illness in homoeopathy is that ailment is a total action of body and mind, the disturbance of the entire organism. Individual organs are not the reason for the disease but the disturbance at internal level (i.e. life force or vital energy). Therefore homoeopathy doesn't believe in prescriptions numerous medicines for numerous afflicted elements of body but instead provides a constitutional remedy which will cover the aggravation of the entire individual.

HERBERT A ROBERTS SPEAKS ABOUT APPROACH FOR DIABETES[44]

We find several appropriate medicines for glucose in urine in the repertories and majority of the homoeopathic medicines listed are very deep acting & have their individual emotional states.

Diabetic patient presents with the subjective symptoms which will guide us to the remedy or he may give a background/history of emotional shock preceding the present affliction that will lead to you a remedy.

The symptoms are clearly marked such that the constitution cannot be overlooked, sometimes it is indicating a constitutional remedy which has not proved to produce sugar imbalance. If the patient improves we are justified by adding this as a clinical note to the existing.

With this medicine if the general well being is raised even though the lower glucose threshold remains the same not to be worried because we may safely rely on the remedy that keeps up general enhancement and not to be too restless over the glucose output.

RICHARD HUGES ON DIABETES[47]

It must always be of high importance, but it is not in the nature of the case and by the confession of its advocates, curative. Sometimes indeed under its use nature relieved of much of her burden, asserts her recuperative power and when the pristine consequences. But too often the diabetic regimen proves but a continuous and most irk some palliative that the least abatement of its rigid restrictions is followed by an increase in the malady and the patient at length succumbs under pulmonary disease, carbuncle, or simple exhaustion of the power of the life. Until we can do more than cut off the supplies, until we can attack the morbid process itself, we cannot consider ourselves in a position to cure diabetes.

When we talk about disease like diabetes, we take in consideration terms of management rather than cure, this is because general management measures like dietary measures and day to day exercise etc., are compulsory, hence along with constitutional homeopathic medicines general management has a very important role in the cure and management of type 2 diabetic patients which not only treats the patients symptoms but also drives the manifestations away and cure the patient from inside. Without a doubt one can demonstrate that homoeopathy is the medicine of future.

MIASMATIC REVIEW

In the beginning of his practice when Dr. Hahnemann started using the law of similia, he got incredible achievement in epidemic and acute infections but he failed hopelessly in a substantial number of chronic diseases. He himself said – "Their start was promising, the continuation less great, the outcome hopeless." Such case made Dr. Hahnemann probe profoundly into the idea of disease and the advancement of the chronic diseases.

Following quite a while of point by point case takings and case analysis, he discovered that almost every one of the patients with chronic ailments had a past history of scabies, syphilis or gonorrhea and majority of the patients were not well since the season of infection. He called these contaminations and the sickness inclination arising from them, miasms. The one rising up out of scabies was called non venereal or psora miasm. The other two were called venereal miasms as they emerged from sexual direct. The one rising from syphilis was known as syphilitic miasma and the one from gonorrhea was known as sycotic miasm.

The term miasm begins from the Greek, signifying 'contamination, taint'.[48] Hippocrates was the first to use it to express his concept of how infectious diseases could be carried by air, water and other sources. The doctor's of Hahnemann's time used the term miasm to indicate the unknown cause of disease which pollutes the whole system so as to produce permanent disease state. They considered syphilis the only existing miasm because the etiology was unknown. They did not consider, the "figwart disease" a miasm because they believed they could cure it by removing the condylomata.

Hahnemann utilized the term miasm in his incredible theory of the sources of chronic disease. He started by isolating by obvious interminable diseases from illnesses that were caused by mechanical or exterior conditions, which could be lightened by altering the nature or way of life style of the patient (Aphorism 77).

But Hahnemann likewise had seen that the best diet, a vigorous constitution and healthy life style could not help to cure a genuine chronic disease. He saw that in spite of such measures, the chronic disease unfurled into new and more awful symptoms, driving unavoidably to a further aggravation and death.

Diet may appear to eliminate a particular expression of disease, such as tumor in the breast, but it cannot eradicate the tendency to produce such a tumor, which Hahnemann credited to the hidden miasm.

Diabetes mellitus includes the pseudopsoric miasm. The pseudopsoric miasm otherwise called tubercular miasm. It is a mix of both syphilitic and psora miasm. Tubercular miasm is commonly depicted by an *"issue child"* i.e. moderate in perception, dull, unfit to keep a line of thought, unsocial, sullen. He/she getting help from hostile foot or axillary perspiration which when suppressed often induces lung inconveniences or some other serious disease. The patient dependably feels better of mental symptoms by an episode of an ulcer. The smallest wound suppurates; the strong inclination is to the arrangement of pustules. As a general rule, the patient is exceptionally clever, sharp observer and a automatic organizer who needs his life constantly occupied but possesses a inactive way of life[48].

INDICATION OF MIASM

As the miasm advance and prevails, weight reduction, depreciation and devastation are the principal sign of this miasm. Different signs are cosmopolitan propensities, rationally sharp but physically feeble. Symptoms are regularly evolving. Fast reaction to any stimuli (e.g. any slightest change of weather or atmosphere). Weakening as opposed to taking appropriate eating routine and drink, inclination to hack and cool effectively, want and needing for unnatural things to eat, with wants and longings for opiates, for example, espresso, tea, tobacco and some different animates have frequently their source in psoric or tubercular miasm. They sometimes have steady craving and eat past their ability to process or they have no craving in the beginning of the day but hunger for different meals.

Miasmatic Discussion on Complications of Diabetes Mellitus

Diabetes mellitus (DM) has a psorosyphilitic foundation. As the syphilitic miasm as winds up transcendent the complexities arises. The intense complications are of the psoric character since they have metabolic aggravations while the chronic complications are related with syphilitic foundation or as a result of mixed miasm. As the solid syphilitic character is going to pulverization and degeneration it prompts blended miasmatic diseases. These sicknesses are progressively hard to cure especially when goes to irreversible changes. At the point when the syphilitic miasm is prevailing in the state of endless intricacies the condition ought to end up fierce. At this stage the individual needs a total miasmatic and restorative treatment.

In homeopathy, we do not fall into the tarp of arguing what is diabetes – the sugar or the vascular changes. We say both are the part of diabetic process. Each patient has a specific constitution. By this, we mean to say that each patient has a specific individual body, mind and disease. That is why different people get diabetes at different times, of differing severity, with different complications, and varying response to same treatment. In Homoeopathy, we attempt to discover a prescription to suit the psychological aura, the physical attributes, also the different inconveniences of the patient. That is why a homoeopath will select a different remedy for different patients with diabetes.

F. Bernoville, "The individual makes his diabetes". This fact leads to individual characteristics, which in their turn leads us to the selection of "His remedy".

But how can we distinguish a patient individually from another? Hahnemann opened a wide panorama of individual pictures in material medica. When we speak of a drug type, we generally mean constitutional remedy of the patient is that drug.

For example, when we say sulphur type, we mean that the constitutional remedy of the patient is sulphur. To understand what we really mean by constitution, let us see what professor E, Minkowski says in this regard.

"The constitution may be defined according to us as the ensemble of characters of the individual performed from the very beginning of the biological existence and transmutable as such hereditary. The notation of this constitution is thus more restricted than that of congeniality".

"On the other hand, constitution is not also super able to 'Hereditary'; at least this word is used in its current meaning. This case belongs to the field of pathology where manifestly exogenous factors come into play. Thus syphilis may be hereditary, but it may not be constitutional in the strictest sense of the term. The predisposition to tuberculosis and many other diatheses may in all probability, be anomalies of constitutional nature".

"The notion of constitution as we have defined above, introduces in the biological becoming (of an individual) he idea of immutability and continuity of the same thing. That continuity and immutability cannot have evidently a mathematical character. They may be adopted to the particular types of the life and to the biological becoming. A constitutional character which was apparent in childhood may not manifest itself apparently after that period but for that reason it will not be les constitutional. In other words, the constitution, which we called the Homoeostatic vital interior, is not completely stagnant. It changes more or less, but at the same time remains more or less constant.

Every homeopath is a 'Holistic Healer'. He therefore is bound to know the 'make up' of man, what constitutes a man and how his organs function.

An essayist clarifies the biochemic treatment of diabetes as follows:

Lactic acid is made out of carbonic acid and water, and should be part up on it's away to the lungs. This is finished by catalytic activity of sodium phosphate in the blood. Any inadequacy of sodium phosphate will cause an unsettling influence in water in the system by enabling an overabundance of lactic acid to accumulate. Nature in her effort to eliminate the water produces the symptoms called diabetes.

But while a absences of sodium phosphate is the guideline reason for diabetes, the chief remedy is sodium phosphate; since it manages the supply of water in the blood. Sodium phosphate additionally emits oxygen, so fundamental for the decay of glucose, and there by keeps its coming to the kidneys as glucose, and also thins, to its ordinary consistency, bile that has moved toward becoming inspissated from an absence of sodium phosphate.

If a case of diabetes has progressed to an impressive degree, the kidneys will wind up excited by the lactic acid and glucose that goes through them. This damage to the tissue of the renal calls upon the red corpuscles of the blood for Iron Phosphate, which will, much of the time, cause a lack in that inorganic salt. Nature, in her endeavors to supply iron, will likely draw on the nerve fluid, potassium phosphate will be too quickly devoured, and the patient experiences from nervous prostration. The treatment, subsequently, for diabetes mellitus is: the phosphates of sodium, potassium and potassium, and the sulphates of sodium. For the incredible functional disturbance of nerve centers caused by the interest made on the blood for the potassium phosphate, delivering sleeplessness and unquenchable craving, potassium phosphate is the dependable remedy. It sets up the useful activity of the pneumogastric nerve and medulla oblongata, which follow up on the lungs and stomach.

For the extraordinary thirst, starvation, and sorrow, gives sodium chloride. It similarly disperses the water in the system and rapidly reestablishes the normal condition.

The phosphates may be combined where at least two or more are indicated, but the sodium sulpahte and sodium chloride should be given separate arrangements. Where there is incredible anorexia and poor hunger calcium phosphate should be given, a little dose after every meal.

As I might want to think, diet cuts however little figure in the treatment of diabetes, aside from as the proposition of sustenance taken. The fundamental object is having the nourishment process. Diabetic patients never gorge/overeat; preferred eat multiple times everyday than overeat once.

Obviously, diet of fat meals or oily food cannot be useful, for the imperative reality that exhausts the liver, causes lack and subsequent thickening of bile and mucus, and once in a while a crystallization of cholestrin in gall duct, which offers rise to symptoms called Hepatic colic, bilious headache or jaundice.

ACCORDING TO STUART CLOSE

By susceptibility we mean the typical quality or capacity of the living life form of getting impressions; the capacity to react to stimuli. Susceptibility is one of the principal attributes of life. Upon it relies up on all working, all vital procedure, physiological and pathological. Digestion, absorption/nutrition, secretion, repair, emission, metabolism and catabolism, and in addition all ailment forms emerging from disease or infection rely on intensity of the living being to respond to explicit upgrades.

ACCORDING TO HAROBERTS

We may characterize susceptibility basically as the response of the organism to internal and external impacts. Individuals are susceptible to disease and contagion in shifting degrees. In investigating susceptibility, we discover it is to a great extent an outflow of a vacuum in the persons. Susceptibility changes in degree in various patients, and at various times in the similar patient. Homoeopathic utilization of a remedy is a delineation of meeting the susceptibility and filling the vacuum that is available in the sick person. Toward the words, the vibrations of the wiped out people/individual call resoundingly to something to address the need.

ACCORDING TO DHAWALE

Susceptibility is an inherited capacity in all living things to react to the stimuli in the environment and respect a fundamental quality that distinguishes the living from the non living.

ACCORDING TO KENT

Susceptibility underlies all virus and all cure. So that cause and cure, the reason of disorder and the cure of ailment knock at the similar entryway. Hahnemann trains that the chronic miasms are the main cause of the acute miasms, there would be no intense. It is in the basic idea of a chronic miasm, to slant man to acute infection and the intense afflictions are as fuel added to an unquenchable fire. Acute diseases then exist from explicit causes participating with susceptibility. On the off chance that there were no adolescents on the earth weak/susceptible to measles we would have no measles. What's more, if there were no chronic miasms there would be no susceptibility.

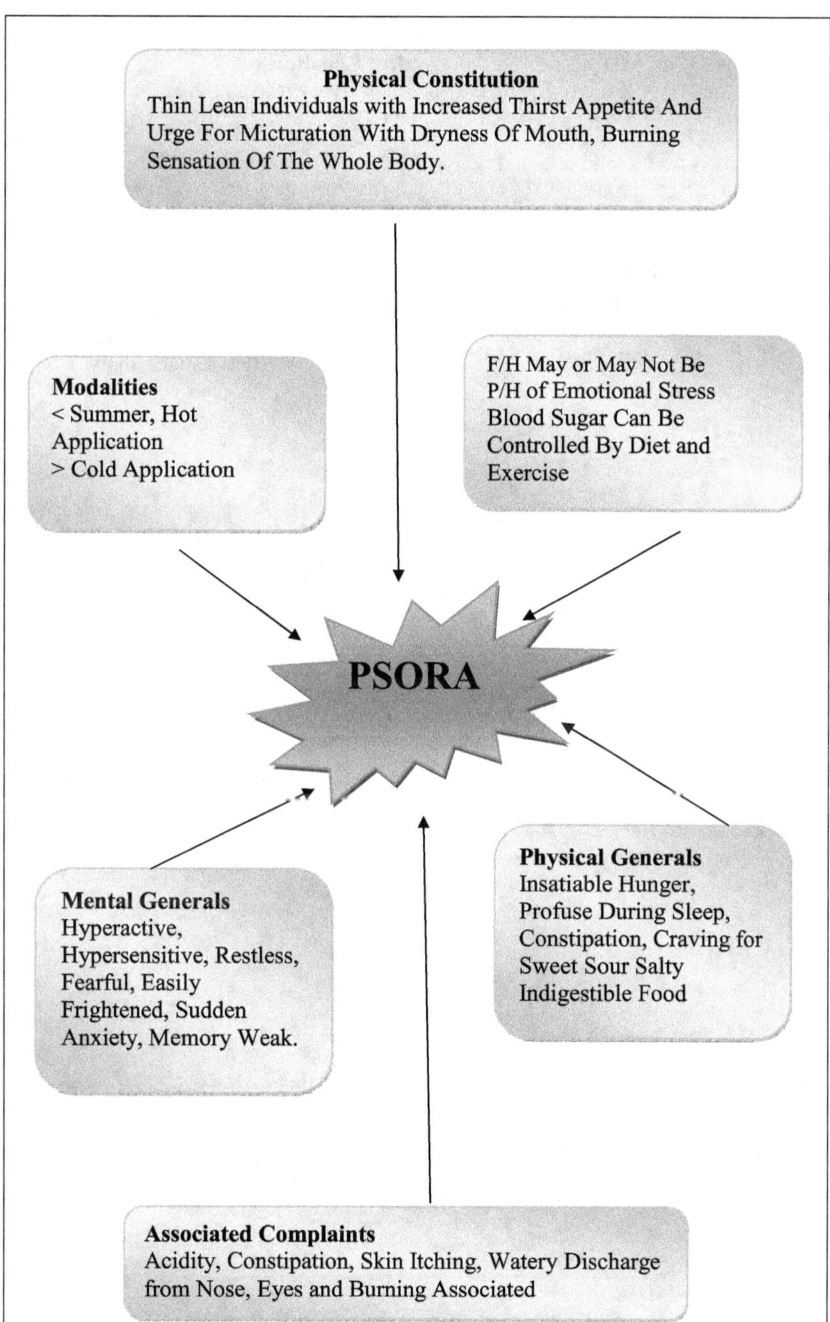

Figure .15 Diagrammatic representation of DM in miasm psora [48]

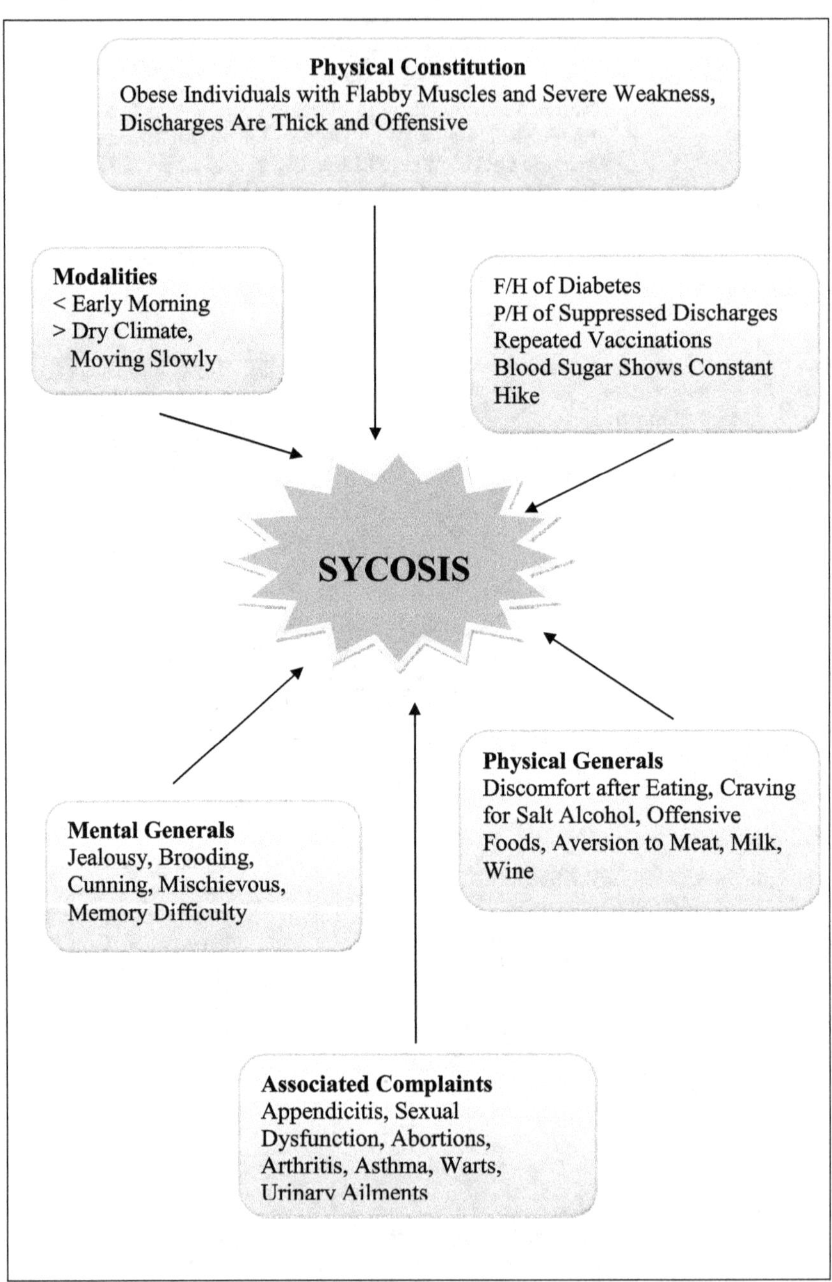

Figure . 16 Diagrammatic representation of DM in miasm sycosis [48]

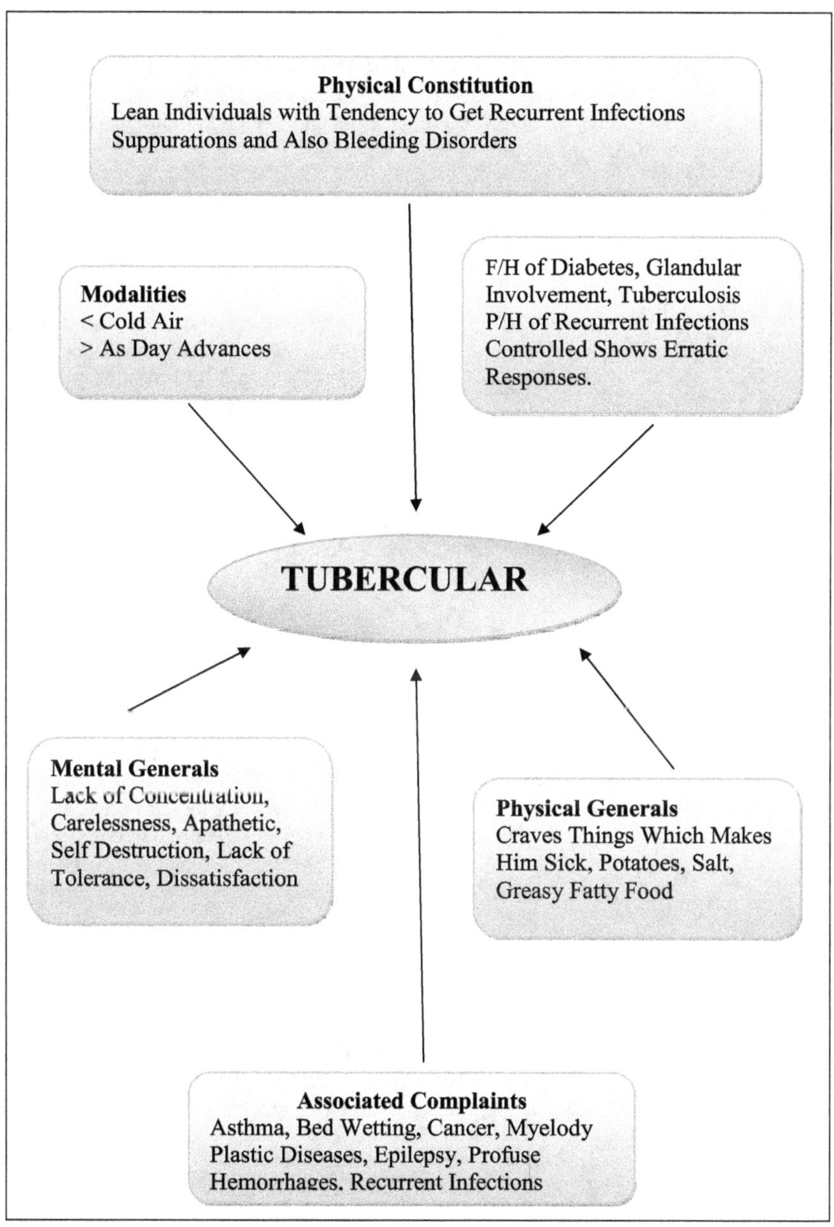

Figure .17 Diagrammatic representation of DM in miasm

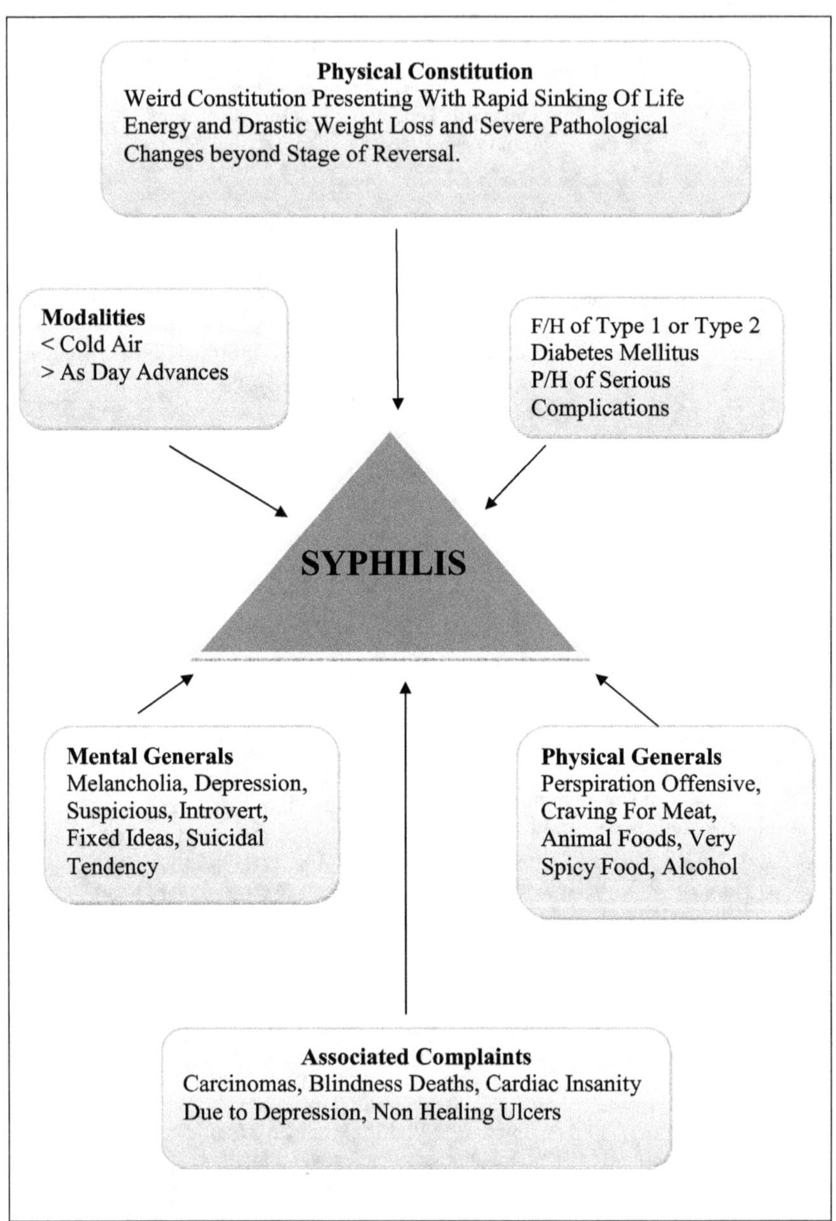

Figure - 18: Diagrammatic representation of DM in miasm Syphilis[48]

THERAPEUTIC APPROACH TO DIABETES MELLITUS ACCORDING TO W.A.DEWEY[49]

- **Lactic Acid;** An exceedingly good remedy in the gastro hepatic variety of diabetes and great out comes regularly decrepit its utilization. It has a fine clinical record. The manifestations are; urination is more and profuse, urine mild yellow and vomiting feeling, thirst, weakness, insatiable appetite and constipating bowels. Dry skin, gastralgia, dry tongue.

- **Bryonia;** Should not be disregarded in this disease. No homoeopathic remedy has dryness of the mouth especially lips as a clinical features of liver disorder more marked than bryonia, and this is regularly one of the important indication of diabetes there is a persevering bitter taste, the patient is lazy, marose and demoralized, thirst may not be extreme not the appetite ravenous, the patient may lose quality through powerlessness to eat.

- **Insulin;** long before the invention of insulin Dr. Jousset. P of paris organized a pancreatic juice on a glycerine basis that he directed to diabetic patients in doses of ten to twenty drops in water in a day and had results adequately good to think about pancreatic juice, orally administered, as a remedy of extraordinary incentive in diabetes.

ACCORDING TO E. A. FARRINGTON

- **Phosphoric acid:** you may see in phosphoric acid a corrosive remedy for diabetes mellitus. The symptoms which drove you to it are, above all else regular, this regular and profuse urination, requiring the patient to rise frequently at night. The urine is frequently milky in appearance. Sometimes it stores jelly like masses, especially in catarrh of the bladder[50].

ACCORDING TO SAMUEL LILIENTHAL:

- **Acetic acid:** Abundant sugar in the urine, enlarged and light yellow colored. Extraordinary thirst, but cold drinks lies overwhelming on stomach; ascites and hydrothorax, oedema pedum; gangrenous ulcers; pale; waxenskin; outrageous prostration.

- **Curare:** Diabetes accutissimus, life threatening; incessant and clear urine, with burrowing, cramp pains within the kidney; mild pain in stomach; mouth fell dry in all times; incredible thirst, particularly evenings and at nigh times; glucose in the urine, great emaciation.

- **Lycopodium:** Crabby and depressed in mind; thirst and hunger steady, but worse at evening times; flatulence; defecation smell in quantity; need of natural; pulmonary rthisis, gauntness; mental, anxious and bodily exhaustion[51].

- **Lycopus virginicus:** diabetes mellitus and insipidus from some unhinging of central nervous system or sympatheticus; plentiful stream of clear urine of great thickness, containing glucose; intense thirst; incredible emaciatin.

- **Moschus:** Insatiable thirst ; great weakening costiveness; impotence; frequent passage of large amounts of saccharine urine, immobile condition of the brain ; obscurity of the sight ; excessive dry in the mouth and rotten taste ; incredible thirst for stimulants; dislike to food; prickling in the dermal area; general fatigue, with coldness everywhere.

- **Ratanhia:** Considerable weakening and weakness; limbs sore and hurting; incredible appetite; insatiable thirst and steady dryness of the mouth; soreness of the kidney; extreme pains in the back, enhanced by motion; excessive urging to urinate, scanty release, passes large light coloured urine.

- **Tarentula** : Profound sadness and anxiety; extraordinary prostration, and pains as if the entire body were wounded; loss of memory and decreased of vision; exceptional thirst; dryness of mouth and lips always that he needs to moisten them with his tongue; insatiable hunger; excessive urination, with brutal pains in the back lower region and completely loss of motion in lower extremities.

- **Thuja:** Glycosuria after a since quite a while ago smothered gonorrhea, want to urinate day and night; needing exchanges with need of hung aches for cool sustenance and drink; urine contains sugar, forms, deposits a brown mucous; debility < mornings[52]

ACCORDING TO S. K. DUBEY:

- **Crarcinocin**: The nosode of carcinocin (generally of breast or stomach). Family history of cancer –Diabetes mellitus, tuberculosis, pernicious anaemia, syphilis or any other degenerative condition is traced –there may be or may not be such history, if symptoms agree carcinocin should be thought of [53].

ACCORDING TO J. D. PATEL

Adrenaline: Kidney: glycosuria.

Metabolism: blood sugar increased

Blood: blood sugar increased.

Characteristic of sarcode: lavish urination with more thirst, this makes the most imperative symptom for their indication in diabetes[54].

ACCORDING TO GEORGE W. CAREY:

The bio chemic homoeopathic remedies in type 2 diabetes vary with the condition present.

- **Kali Phos:** Absence of this salt which is the main factor in expediting on the disease, and it is n't until the sensory system has been reestablished to normal that the pancreas can be required to work normally once more. Dr. Schuessler says that may be kali phos and calc. sulph may likewise fill in as diabetic remedies; while Dr. Walker gave Ferrum phos and nat. phos as an addition tonic with good results, Nat sulph: was also given as the chief remedy in each case.

- **Nat Sulph:** Deranged liver condition and the abundance of water in the frame work call for nat sulph. An imperative cure in all phases of diabetes. Excessive secretion of urine.

- **Fer Phos:** diabetes, when there is an enlivened pulse or pain heat or blockage in any part of the system, as an intercurrent or interchange/alternate remedy.

- **Calc Phos:** Polyurea, with shortcoming, much thirst, dry mouth and tongue; overweight, indented abdomen, salt and craves bakon . Glycosuria, when lungs are involved

- **Kali Mur:** Unreasonable and glucose urine, extraordinary weakness and sleepiness.

- **Nat Mur:** The dreadful thirst and fast emaciation show an unequal circulation of water in the system. Extraordinary debility and melancholy[55].

ACCORDING TO WILLIUM BOERIKE

- **Abroma Augusta:** profuse and frequent mictuririton day and night (polyurea) dryness of the mouth and great thirst; desire to drink after micturition which relieves thirst; micturation leads to fatigue; fishy like smell in urine; a slight dregs; diabetes mellitus; white ulcers at the mouth of prepuce caused by over passage of glucose in urine.

- **Syzygium Jambolanum:** Has a prompt effect of expanding the blood glucose, glycosuria results. An extremely helpful remedy in diabetes mellitus. No other remedy causes such stamped level of reduction and disappearance of glucose in urine. Thorny heat in the upper piece of the body; little red pimples itch savagely. Extraordinary thirst, starvation and weakness. Diabetic ulceration old ulcers of skin.

- **Uranium nit:** causes glycosuria and polyurca. Copious micturation. Dieresis. Incontinence of urine. Diabetes (mellitus and insipidus). Starvation and tympanitis. Burning in urethra with exceptionally acrid urine.

- **Gymnema sylvestre:** is almost specific for diabetes mellitus. Diminishes glucose in the urine, patients put on weight, appetite improves; assumes healthy look. Plentiful micturition loaded with glucose; extreme weakness subsequent to passing substantial amount of urine. Color of the urine is light white with high explicit gravity.

- **Role of Cephalandra Indica Q** in the administration of diabetes mellitus as an extra on medicine along with convention anti diabetics. Therefore cephalandra indica mother tincture could oversee fasting blood sugar (F.B.S) level more to that post prandial blood sugar (PPBS) level. – A study directed by C.C.R.H. New Delhi, India[56].

ACCORDING TO A.C. COWPERTHWAITE:

- Kali brom: Diabetes, urine stacked with glucose. Urine copious, pale, watery.

- Helonis: has been found particularly useful in disease, diabetes mellitus (type 2), with gauntness, fretfulness, thirst, sadness[57].

ACCORDING TO W.M.H.BURT:

- **Ether:** sulphuric ether. Chemical preparation: alcoholic attenuations. Urinary organs: Diabetes –no remedy produces glycosuria more markedly than ether; and it may prove one of our most useful remedies for this fearful malady[58].

ACCORDING TO K. N. MATHUR:

- **Lecithin:** urine contains phosphates, sugar and albumin. Brain fag, neurasthenia and insomnia, forgetful. Tired weak, short breath and loss of flesh.

- **Pancreatin:** diabetes with lientric diarrhea, thin diabetics, pancreatic diabetes.

- **Senna:** urine contains sugar, acetone, oxalates and phosphates, prostration, fainting and constipation with colic and flatulence[59].

REPRESENTATION OF DIABETES MELLITUS IN VARIOUS HOMOEOPATHIC REPERTORIES

ACCORDING TO S. R. PHATAK

Diabetes Mellitus: Arg-Met; Ars; Bov; Carb-Veg; Chion; HELL; *Iris;* Kreos; LYC; *Nat- Mur;* PHOS-AC; PLUMB; Ran-B;Sep; Scil; *Sulph;* TAREN; TERB; Thuja; URAN-NIT

BOILS, Successive With: Nat-Phos[60]

ACCORDING TO JOHN HENRY CLARKE

Diabetes: Acet Ac, Alumn, Amm Act, Anthraco, Arg Met, Arg Nit, Arn, Ars, Br, Asapr, Bov, Calc, Calc P, Carb Ac, Coloch, Coloc, Cur, Eup Perf, Fer Ph, Fer M, Hyndrng, Iod, Kali Ac, Kali Br, Lac Ac, Lyco, Mag S, Med, Mosch, Murx, Nat M, Nat P, Nat S, Phos Ac, Rat, Sanic, Squill, Sec, Sil, Stict, Sulph, Sulp Ac, Syzyg, Tarax, Tril, Urca.

Insipidus: Apoc., Kali N, Squil, Uran N.

Diabetes Mellitus: Op., Uran-N.

Pancreatic: Iris, Pancr[61]

ACCORDING TO BOERICKE OSSCAR

DIABETES SUGAR; Acet-Ac., Adren., Am.Act., Arg-N., Arist., Arsa., Ars al Br Ars I., *Auru.,* Aur-Me., Bell., *Bor-Ac.,* Bov., *Bry.,* Caps., Carb-Ac., Cean., *Cham.,*Chel., Chim., Chion., *Coca., Cod.,* Colch., *Crot-H.,* Cupr-Ar., *Cur.,* Eup Per., *Fel.,* Fer-I., Fer- M., Fl- Ac, Glon., Glyc., Grind., *Hell.,Helon.,* Iod., *Iris.,* Kali Ac., Kali-Br., *Kreos., Lac- Ac.,*Lach., Lec.,Lyc., Lycps.V., Lyss.,Morp.,*Mosch.* Murx., Nat-M., *Nat S.* ,Nit Aci., Nux vom., Op., *Pancr.,* Phase., *Phos-Ac., Phos., Phlor.,Pic-Ac.,* Plb., Plb-I., Podo., *Rhus-A.,* Sec., Sil., Squil., Stry-Ar., Sulph., *Syzg.,* Tarent., Tarax., Ter., *Uran-N.,* UreaN., Vanad., Vince[62].

ACCORDING TO BOGER C M

Saccharine : Amyl-N., *Arg.,* **Ars.,** *Aur., Bar-C., Carb-V.,*Chin., *Colo.,*Con., Curar., *Helon., Kali-B.,* Kali-C., *Kali-P.,* Kreos., *Led., Lyco.,*Mag-C., Meph., *Merc., Mur-*Ac., Phos., PHOS-*AC., Pic-Ac., Plb.,* Ran-B., *Sec-C.,*Sep., **Sulp.,** Tarx., **Thuj.,** Zinc[63].

ACCORDING TO FREDERICK SCHROYENS

GENERALS: Diabetes mellitus (urine sugar)

Abrom A., Adren., All S., Allox., Alum., Am Act., Anthraco., Apoc., Arg Met., Arist M., Ars., *Ars Br.,* Asc c., Aspr., Aur., Aur M N., *Bor Ac.,* Bov., Calc., Calc ph, calca sil, cantha, carb ac, carb Veg, carci, card m, carl, causti, ceph In, cheli, chim, chion, coffe, colocy, coni, cop, cortico, cortiso, calc ph, cantha, Cub., Cupra, Curu, Eup Pe, Ferr I, Ferr M, Fer Ph, Fl Ac., Flor Ph., Gal Ac, Glyc, Gymne., Hed, Helon, Hydrang, Insu, Inul, Iodi, Iris v, Kali Act, Kali Bro, Kali Ph, Kreosa, Lac Aci., Lac D, Lacha, Lyco, Lycps V, Mag Ph, Mag S, Meda., Meny, Mercu, Merc D., Morph, Mosch, Murex, Nat Mu., Nat Ph, Nat Su, Nit Aci., Nux Ve, Opi, Oxyg, Pancr, Phase, Phosp, Plant, Podop, Ran Bu, Rata, Rhus a, Rhus Tox, Sacch L, Sanic, Sepi, Ser ng, Sili, Spong, Squill, Stict, Strot C, Sul Ac, Sulph., Syzg, Tarentu, Ter, Trerebin, thuja, thry, Uran Ni, Urea n, Vanad.

Accompanied by:

-abscesses : ars.

-acne: ars-br.

-albuminuria: helon

-Alcoholism (see MIND-Alcoholism-diabetes) Mind: Alcoholism: diabetes; with: med, nux-v.

-Appetite-ravenous: kali-p., lac-ac., rat., uran-n.

-arteriosclerosis : aur, chlorpr, plb, syzg.

-boils: *anthr, anthraco,* arn, ars, chorpr., ins., nat-p., ph-ac.

-carbuncles: ars, *crot-h.,* gymne, ins, kreos, *lach.*

-constipation: carl, lac-d, nat-s.

-diarrhea:ars, gal-ac, kali-act, pancr.

-dropsy: acet-ac, kali-act

-eczema: ins

-emaciation: ars, ars-br, cupr, cur, helon, kali-br, lac-d, merc, nat-s, pancr, ph-ac, rat, tarent, uran-met[64].

ACCORDING TO BTPB

URINE – Sacchainre

aml-ns. Arg-met. ARS. Aur. Bar-ca. Carb-ve. china. Coloc. con. cur. Helo. Kali-bic. kali-c. Kali-p. kreos. Led. Lyc. mag-c. meph. Merc. Mur-ac. NAT MU. Nat su. nit-aci. PH-ACI. phosp. Pic-aci. Plb. ran-bu. Sec. sep. SULPH. tarax. THUJ. zinc.

Lower Extremities - Numbness - foot

acon. ambra. ang. ant-cr arg-ni. arni. ars alb. asar. bry. CAUST. cham. cocc. con. graph. kali-bi. merc. NUX VO. opi. Pho aci. phosp. plati. plb. rhus-t. sec. stront-c. thuj[65].

Skin and Exterior Body - Gangrene - moist, (humid)

Brom, CHIN, hell, vip[66].

ACCORDING TO KENT

URINE – sugar

Acetac, all s, arg m, ars, benzac, bov, carb v, chin, COLCH, cup, HELON, kali p, lac, LYC, mag s, nit ac, podo, sil, TARENT, thuja, uran, zinc [67].

DEFINITION OF THE STUDY SUBJECT:

Subjects are considered on the basis of clinical presentations, a systemic history taking, complete clinical examination and necessary investigation.

PRIMARY SOURCE:

- The subject for this examination was assembled from O.P.D. (outpatient department) and I.P.D. (in patient department) of Sri Ganganagar homoeopathic medical college, Hospital Post Graduate Center, Sri Ganganagar, Rajasthan, India.

- Peripheral outpatient of Sri Ganganagar Homoeopathic Medical College, Hospital Post Graduate Center, Sri Ganganagar, Rajasthan.

INCLUSION CRITERIA:

- Patients are both genders, regardless of financial status.

- The example cases with age amass between 31 to 70 years.

- Diagnostic criteria are based mainly on clinical presentation and blood examination of type 2 diabetes mellitus patients.

EXCLUSIVE CRITERIA:

- Patients over 70 years and below 31 years old with type 2 diabetes mellitus.

- Serious complications.

- Inflammatory changes.

- Diabetes associated with other systemic diseases which are on active treatment.

- Pregnant or lactating during the study.

- Diagnosed with deficiency in glucose-6-phosphate

- Unable to speak the Hindi and English language were excluded, as the consultation for this research was facilitated in English.

STUDY DESIGN:

Non control trial based upon purposive sampling method. The cases are selected according to inclusion and exclusion criteria. Case taking was done according to scheme of model case performa, with special emphasis to ascertain the fallowing points.

Presenting complaints:

The complaints were noted in chronological order of appearance with duration.

History of the presenting complaints:

The presenting complaints along with the history of location, duration, onset, character of pain and associated complaints were recorded.

Past History:

The past history was also considered in detail in the chronological order.

Family History:

A detailed family history was taken, to find out the incidence of degenerative disease or any other acute or chronic disease prevalent in the family on both sides of the parents or immediate relations.

Personal History:

As homoeopathy treats the patient and not the disease in the patient, for constitutional prescribing the personal history with special emphasis on mind, thermals, desires, aversion, thirst, appetite, dreams, sleep etc., was recorded in detail.

General physical examination:

A general physical examination of the patient to ascertain the vital parameters and basic data of the patient was done in all case.

Systemic examination:

Detail systemic examination of central nervous system, cardiovascular system and gastro intestinal system and skin is carried out. In case any positive findings are present they are recorded.

Investigations:

The following investigations are carried out in cases of type 2 diabetes mellitus.

- urine analysis: Urine sugar in FBS and PPBS

     Urine sugar in RBS (if required)

     Microscopic test to eliminate diabetic nephropathy.

- Blood glucose: FBS, PPBS and RBS.

- Other   HbA1C, lipid profile, thyroid and urea.

     ECG, Chest radiograph, eye screening (if required).

Diagnosis:

The conclusion of type 2 diabetes mellitus is made based on clinical introductions and examinations/investigations.

Follow up:

Follow up was done till the patient was relieved of the complaints initially once in fifteen days and later as per the requirement of the patients.

STEPS OF HOMOEOPATHIC PRESCRIPTION:

Patient should be treated depending on the individual case, constitution of the patient and on the basis of totality of symptoms. Homoeopathic constitutional medicines are given according to the patient's susceptibility and were repeated on requirement.

Analysis of symptoms:

After detailed case taking, the symptoms of the patient were grouped in to various categories like mental generals, physical generals and particulars.

Evaluation:

After analyzing the symptoms in to various categories, the symptoms were evaluated and according to the order of their importance.

Repertorisation:

Cases were repertorised as per the need of the cases. The most similar drug was selected.

Selection of remedy:

The most similar drug was selected from the reportorial result with the help of Materia Medica.

Potency and repetition:

The indicated medicine was given in an appropriate potency, basing on the susceptibility of the patient at the time of every prescription.

Statistical Methods Employed:

Chi square test of independence:

The purpose of using this statistical tool for result analysis was that firstly this was a prospective study, there was no comparative study, and secondly the subjects undertaken were 30 in number so this statistical tool would prove effective for result analysis.

Ethical clearances in the study:

The ethical clearance was obtained from the institution for the clinical study on human subjects. Ethical qualities were taken up carefully according to ICMR rules for biomedical research on human subjects.

The result of treatment was based on:

The result of treatment was interpreted of those cases, whose follow up was obtained until the end of the study.

The following criteria were fixed to know the results of the treatments, depending upon the type of response from different patients.

- o General condition of the patient.
- o Reduction in severity/frequency of symptoms.
- o If any other complications.

Every one of the criteria ought to be satisfied for somewhere around a half year to mark the case as improved, not improved and dropped out.

Result Criteria:

The results were categorized into 3 categories based on the above criteria.

➤ Improved:

Feeling of mental, physical well being with marked decrease in the intensity and severity of symptoms for a period less than 6 months and normal/above normal FBS, PPBS count.

➤ Not improved:

Recurrent attacks of diabetes continuing with persistent signs even after defined period of treatment.

➤ Recovered:

Feeling of mental, physical well being with marked decrease in the intensity and severity of symptoms for a period more than 6 months and normal/above normal FBS, PPBS count.

TABLE 1: DISTRIBUTION OF THE TYPE 2 DIABETES ACCORDINGTO AGE

The incidence of type 2 diabetes mellitus found in different age groups is shown in the table given below.

Sl. No	Age of the patient	No. of Cases	Percentage (%)
1	31-40	4	13.33
2	41-50	15	50.00
3	51-60	4	13.33
4	61-70	7	23.33
	Total	30	100

As shown in the above table, the maximum age incidence of 50.00 % was between 41-50 Years is 15 cases and minimum age incidence of 13.33 % was observed in 31-40 years of age in 4 cases. 7 cases between age group of 61-70 years showed 23.33 % and 4 cases in 51-60 years age group shows 13.33% incidence [Vide table no:01].

TABLE 2: DISTRIBUTION OF THE TYPE 2 DIABETES ACCORDING TO SEX

The incidence of type 2 diabetes mellitus found in different sex group is shown in the table given below.

Sl. No	Age of the patient	No. of Cases	Percentage (%)
1	Male	19	63.27
2	Female	11	36.63
	Total	30	100

The table shows the statistical study of sex incidence in 30 patients. The study shows maximum sex incidence in male i.e. 19 cases accounting to 63.27% of the total and minimum incidence of 36.63% of the total who were female in 11 cases [Vide table no: 02].

TABLE 3: DISTRIBUTION OF THE TYPE 2 DIABETES ACCORDING TO THE OCCUPATIONAL

The incidence of type 2 diabetes mellitus found in different occupational incidents is shown in the table given below.

Sl. No	Occupation	No. of Cases	Percentage (%)
1.	House Wife	9	30.00
2.	Bank Employee	3	10.00
3.	Businessmen	4	13.33
4.	Govt. Employee	3	10.00
5.	Teachers	7	23.33
6.	Farmer	2	6.67
7.	Maid	2	6.67
	Total	30	100

Type 2 diabetes mellitus was found with greater incidence in 9 cases making 30.00% among house wife, the next highest were 7 cases making 23.33% among teachers and business class were 4 cases making 13.33% followed by bank employees and government employees each constituted 3 cases making 10% maid and farmer constituted 2 cases each making 6.67% [vide table no: 03].

TABLE 4: DISTRIBUTION OF THE TYPE 2 DIABETES ACCORDING TO THE PHYSICAL COMPLAINTS

The incidence of type 2 diabetes mellitus found in different physical complaints is shown in the table given below.

Sl. No	Physical Complaints	No. of Cases	Percentage (%)
1	Recurrent sore throat	4	13.33
2	Sneezing	2	6.66
3	Muscle cramps	2	6.66
4	Joint pains	1	3.33
5	Constipation	3	10.00
6	Back ache	1	3.33
7	Sinusitis	2	6.66
8	Eczema	3	10.00
9	Coryza, Nose block	1	3.33
10	Haemorrhoids	3	10.00
11	Head ache	2	6.66
12	Heart burn	2	6.66
13	Distended Abdomen, Flatulence	1	3.33
14	Bronchitis	3	10.00

The study showed that 4 patients had recurrent sore throat accounting to 13.33%, 2 patients had sneezing accounting to 6.66%, 2 patients had muscle cramps accounting to 6.66%, 1 patients had joint pains accounting to 3.33%, 3 patients had constipation accounting to 10.00%, 1 patients had back ache accounting to 3.33%, 2 patients had sinusitis accounting to 6.66 %, 3 patients had eczema accounting to 10.00 %, 1 patients had coryza, nose block accounting to 3.33 %, 3 patients had haemorrhoids accounting to 10.00 %, 2 patients had headache accounting to 6.66 %, 2 patients had heartburn accounting to 6.66%. 1 patients had flatulence and distended abdomen accounting to 3.33%. 3 patients had bronchitis accounting to 10.00 %.

TABLE 5: DISTRIBUTION OF THE TYPE 2 DIABETES ACCORDING TO THE PAST HISTORY

The incidence of type 2 diabetes mellitus found in different past history is shown in the table given below.

Sl. No	Past History	No. of Cases	Percentage (%)
1	Constipation	5	16.66
2	Bronchial asthma	3	10.00
3	Malaria	3	10.00
4	Haemorrhoids	3	10.00
5	Allergic bronchitis	2	6.66
6	Jaundice	2	6.66
7	Tonsillitis	2	6.66
8	Pulmonary TB	3	10.00
9	Inguinal hernia	1	3.33
10	Typhoid	3	10.00
11	Pneumonia	2	6.66
12	Sinusitis	1	3.33

The study showed that 5 cases had constipation accounting to 16.66%, 3 patients had bronchial asthma accounting to 10%, 3 patients had malaria in their past history accounting to 10%. 3 patients had haemrrhoids accounting to 10%. 2 patients had allergic bronchitis accounting to 6.66%, 2 patients had jaundice accounting to 66.6%, 2 patients had tonsillitis accounting to 6.66%, 3 patients had pulmonary tuberculosis & typhoid accounting to 10.00%, 1 patient had hernia & sinusitis accounting to 3.33%. 2 patients had pneumonia accounting to 6.66%.

TABLE 6: DISTRIBUTION OF THE TYPE 2 DIABETES ACCORDING TO THE FAMILY HISTORY

The incidence of type 2 diabetes mellitus found in different other family history is

shown in the table given below.

Sl. No	Family History	No. of Cases	Percentage (%)
1	Presence of F/H of DM	18	60.00
2	Absent of F/H of DM	12	40.00

After the cases been worked out I found that many of the cases in their background

presented with a family history of diabetes mellitus in previous generation recent or

remote out of 30 cases 18 (60.00%) cases presented with family history of diabetes

mellitus where as 12 (40.00%) of cases did not presented with the family history [vide

table no: 6].

TABLE 7: DISTRIBUTION OF THE TYPE 2 DIABETES ACCORDING TO THE PRESCRIBED REMEDIES

The incidence of type 2 diabetes mellitus found in different other prescribed remedies is shown in the table given below.

Sl. No	Remedies	No. of Cases	Percentage (%)
1.	Kali carb	7	23.33
2.	Lycopodium	6	20.00
3.	Acid Phos	3	10.00
4.	Nux vomica	1	3.33
5.	Kali phos	2	6.67
6.	Pulsatilla	5	16.67
7.	Nat sulph	3	10.00
8.	Calc carb	3	10.00
	TOTAL	30	100

In this study, kali carb is frequently indicated as prescribed remedies among 7 cases which is 23.33%, Followed by lycopodium in 6 cases making 20% and pulsatilla in 5 cases which is 16.67%. Followed by acid phos, nat sullph, calc carb indicated in 3 cases showing 10% of the incidence. Kali phos in 2 cases making 6.67% of the incidence and Nux vom are indicated once in each case making 3.33% of the incidence [vide table no: 07].

TABLE 8: DISTRIBUTION OF THE TYPE 2 DIABETES ACCORDING TO THE MIASMATIC BACK GROUND

The incidence of type 2 diabetes mellitus found in miasmatic back ground is shown in the table given below.

Sl. No	Miasms	No. of Cases	Percentage (%)
1	Pseudo Psora	7	23.33
2	Psoro Syphilitic	20	66.66
3	Psora	3	10.00
	TOTAL	30	100

Statistical study was done the results of 30 cases. Out of 30 cases, 7 cases (23.33%) are Pseudo Psora, 20 cases (66.66 %) are Psora syphilitic, 3 cases (10.00 %) are Psora [vide table no:08].

TABLE 9: DISTRIBUTION OF THE TYPE 2 DIABETES ACCORDING TO RESULT

The incidence of type 2 diabetes mellitus found in different other result is shown in the table given below.

Sl. No	Results	No. of Cases	Percentage (%)
1	Recovered	12	40.00
2	Improved	10	33.33
3	Not improved	8	26.66
	TOTAL	30	100

Statistical study was done the results of 30 cases. Out of 30 cases, 12 cases (40.00%) were recovered, 10 cases (33.33%) were improved and 8 cases (26.66%) were did not show any improvement [vide table no: 09].

STATISTICAL STUDY

Chi Square test of independence:

Step-1

Null Hypothesis (H_0): Homoeopathic medicines not helpful in the management of type 2 diabetes mellitus.

Alternative Hypothesis (H_1): Homoeopathic medicines may helpful in the management of type 2 diabetes mellitus.

Step- 2

Contingency table

Results / Sex	Improved	recovered	Not improved	Total
Males	09	04	06	19
Females	01	08	02	11
Total	10	12	8	30

Step – 3

Calculation.

Expected Frequency of individual cells =

$$\text{Expected Frequency of individual cells} = \frac{\text{Total Row X Total Colum}}{\text{Whole total}}$$

$$E_a = 19X\ 10\ /\ 30 \quad = 6.3$$
$$E_b = 19X\ 12\ /\ 30 \quad = 7.6$$
$$E_c = 19X\ 8\ /\ 30 \quad = 5.0$$
$$E_d = 11X\ 10\ /30 \quad = 3.6$$
$$E_e = 11X\ 12\ /\ 30 \quad = 4.4$$
$$E_f = 11X\ 8\ /\ 30 \quad = 2.9$$

Step – 4
Calculations of χ^2

$$\chi^2 a = (O-E)^2 / E = (9-6.3)^2 / 6.3 = 1.15$$
$$\chi^2 b = (O-E)^2 / E = (4-7.6)^2 / 7.6 = 1.70$$
$$\chi^2 c = (O-E)^2 / E = (6 - 5.0)^2 / 5.0 = 0.2$$
$$\chi^2 d = (O-E)^2 / E = (1 - 3.6)^2 / 3.6 = 1.87$$
$$\chi^2 e = (O-E)^2 / E = (8 - 4.4)^2 / 4.4 = 2.94$$
$$\chi^2 f = (O-E)^2 / E = (2 - 2.9)^2 / 2.9 = 0.27$$

step – 5   Total of $\chi^2 = 8.13$

step - 6   Degree of Freedom (D.F.) $= (\text{Column} - 1)(\text{Row} - 1)$

$$= (3 - 1)(2 - 1)$$

$$= 2 \times 1 = 2$$

Step – 7   Table value of χ^2 at d.f 2 is 5.991

Step – 8   Inference is calculated value is 8.13 greater than the table value.

P is 0.01672402

Step – 9   Conclusion.

The null hypothesis formulated in the beginning of the study " Homoeopathic medicines may not be helpful in the management of type 2 diabetes mellitus" is rejected and the alternative hypothesis homoeopathic medicines is helpful in the management of type 2 diabetes mellitus" from statistical analysis of the cases is accepted.

The present study carried over 30 cases that fulfilled the consideration criteria to study the efficacy of homoeopathic remedies in the management of type 2 diabetes mellitus.

Most common victims of type 2 diabetes are elderly people. As in my study out of 30 patients, the highest incidence of type 2 diabetes mellitus was observed in the age group 41-50 years followed by 61-70 years and least 51-60 and 31-40 years. Hence the patients from 40 and above are most affected with type 2 diabetes mellitus prominently observed in elderly people and incidences are relatively reduced in young adults. (Vide table no.1 and graph no.1). In my study the above trend shows, the most common victim to type 2 diabetes mellitus are, males that are 63.27% and rest 36.63% are females (vide table no.2 and graph no.2).

In order to ascertain the kind of occupation that predisposes or facilitates the sustenance of type 2 diabetes mellitus and also to know that occupation where it was commonly prevalent the occupational history of the patients was considered. Housewives (9 cases) were found to be most vulnerable group in the population, as they comprise 30.00%. As this study was conducted in a tropical and developing country, India where the more of life, various habits, sedentary life styles, mental tension and lack of health education to prevent diabetes mellitus, are mainly responsible for type 2 diabetes mellitus. This is very well documented, as incidence of type 2 diabetes mellitus is higher in developing countries because of change in lifestyle, various habits, sedentary habits and mental tension it affects both sexes and in 31-40 years and above age groups.

Out of 30 subjects, 4 cases are business man, 2 farmers, 7 teachers, 3 Govt employees, 3 bank employees and 2 maids are observed during my study. (Vide table no 3 and graph no 3).

As the clinical study (research thesis) was carried out with 30 subjects, respective changes were noted during the treatment. Initially on the first visit, the whole case was being taken with measurement of blood glucose content using investigations such as random blood sugar, fasting blood sugar, PPBS and HbA1c. All the patients were educated about diet and regimen and balance sugar pre diet. Patients were told to review once in 15 days and later once in month. As in my study homoeopathic polycrest/constitutional remedy was prescribed with a view of aims and destinations of presenting study. Kali carb is most frequently indicated in 7 out of 30 cases making 23.33% of incidence, lycopodium in 6 cases making 20% incidence, pulsatila is indicated in 5 cases making 16.67%, acid phos, nat sulp, cal carb 3 cases marking 10.00%, kali phos in 2 case marking 6.67%, nux vom 1 case marking 3.33% . Some of the cases showed improvements and few no improvements because in some few cases, the totality might have not been accurately created where in other few cases, there were patients who could not be affordable for doing the investigation every time or some other personal reasons which were not came for follow up [vide table no: 7].

As in my study it was observed that out of 30 cases 18 cases which is of 60.00% of incidence shown the familial background of type 2 diabetes mellitus and 12 cases making 40.00% incidence showed the absence of familial history. Strongly indicating the hereditary traits of type 2 diabetes mellitus [vide table no: 06].The cases results fixed were recovered, improved and not improved the outcome of the study in among 30 cases 10 (33.33%) cases have improved, 12 (40.00%) cases have recovered and 8 (26.66%) cases not improved [vide table no: 09]. Out of 8 not improved cases, they were case no 3 SD, cases no 5 BSM, case no 8 CJS, case no 10 SSC, case no 15 NAJ, case no 17 VSV, case no 19 NHP , case no 22 NAJ.

After the study, I conclude, the commonness of type 2 diabetes mellitus is most common metabolic deficiency throughout the world that negatively impacts on health and development. We must move beyond current ideology, and learn how to better asses those populations at risk for the development of type 2 diabetes mellitus regardless of the concurrent medical conditions. Evidence based practice guidelines need to include diagnostic measures that identify the change in blood glucose status early to avoid progression of type 2 diabetes mellitus, and specific management goals that include treatment strategies including what constitutes a favorable response to blood glucose therapy. Homoeopathy by addressing all causes of individual and their complete set of symptoms through the holistic approach is observed to be useful to other system of treatment chiefly in the diseases like type 2 diabetes mellitus.

Homoeopathy treatment is essentially based on the constitutional approach targeting the fundamental cause (miasm) and restoring the vital principle back to normal, there by cure/improvement (in cases of manageable diseases like diabetes mellitus) of the disease occurs. In other system of drug, the treatment of type 2 diabetes mellitus is for the most part palliative treatment as opposed to corrective. They commonly use insulin therapies and oral hypoglycemic agents which have their own side effects.

A few people have reactions, for example, low glucose. Other side effects of insulin treatment is swelling, redness or itching at the site of infusions, compounding of the diabetic retinopathy, changes in appropriation of muscle to fat ratio (lipodystrophy), allergic reactions sodium retention and general body swelling, a kind of chest inconvenience dyspnea and cough, weight loss reduction and weakness and muscle torment. So by taking homoeopathic medication helps in keeping the blood glucose level in normal.

Here in this study few cases allopathic medication was gradually tapered and many were strictly on homoeopathic treatment alone.

Homoeopathic remedies are boon especially for those who are having co-morbid conditions, and to those who are likely to have severe side effects from allopathic medicines. Our prescriptions expel the sickness side effects as well as enhance over all status of the patient.

By homoeopathic medicines we can recover/improve type 2 diabetes mellitus with no symptoms through the natural secretion of insulin. In old age and sensitive individuals where intestinal gut becomes sensitive to insulin therapy causing vomiting, abdominal fullness, mal absorption of Vit B12, diarrohea.

Homoeopathic medicine along with general management in the form of diet charts and exercise guidelines can do the best to the patient and their effective application has been assessed on subsequent follow ups.

LIMITATION:

- Less number of cases.
- Time bound study i.e. 2 ½ years.
- Patients registering only to Sri Ganganagar homoeopathic medical college & hospital OPD, IPD and peripheral OPD are taken.

RECOMMENDATION:

Further study to be completed to discover the efficacy in detail.

Diabetes mellitus is a metabolic disorder portrayed by hyperglycemia due to absolute or relative insufficiency of insulin, insulin resistance or both. There is unsettling influence of meddle person digestion chiefly showing as ceaseless hyperglycemia. There is an encouraging momentum where in the lay pubic has become more aware of homeopathy. The manifestations of type 2 diabetes mellitus can be great treated with homoeopathic medicines.

The present clinical study has been a modest effort on my part to explore and understand type 2 diabetes mellitus and its manifestations, which afflicts the subjects and sufferings about an array of symptoms to understand the miasmatic background that envelops the diseased man and to understand the efficacy of homoeopathic remedies in the treatment of type 2 diabetes mellitus. My present clinical study has been an encouraging and successful one in fulfilling the objectives.

30 different cases of type 2 diabetes mellitus which satisfies the inclusion and exclusion criterion irrespective of the sex, age, occupational, past history, family histories were considered to study efficacy of homoeopathic remedies in management of type 2 diabetes mellitus.

In my study, it appears that there is wide scope of homoeopathic management in type 2 diabetes mellitus. The highest age incidence found was between 41-50 years 15 cases (50%), followed by 61-70 years 7 cases (23.33%), 31-40 years and 51-60 years each making 4 cases (13.33%) and sex incidence was highest in male with 19 cases (63.27%) and females 11 cases (36.63%).

Occupationally, the highest prevalence was found in house wife's 9 cases (30%) followed by teacher were 7 cases (23.33%), businessman 4 cases (13.33%), bank employees and government employees were 3 cases each (10.00%), former and maid were 2 cases each (6.67%).

In family history presence of diabetes mellitus was found to be highest i.e. 18 cases (60.00%) and absences of family history were found to be 12 cases (40.00%). Among remedies the highest indicated was kali carb in 7 cases (23.33%), lycopodium was 6 cases (20.00%), pulsatilla was 5 cases (16.67%), acid phos followed by nat sulph, calc carb in 3 cases (10.00%), kali phos was 2 cases (6.67%) and nux vomica was indicated in one case (3.33%).

The results are divided in to three types:

- Recovered

- Improved

- Not improved

The result was analyzed for six months after the treatment which showed considerable recovered in signs and symptoms and general feeling of prosperity in the patient. This was possible by acute phase remedies and constitutional remedies.

Recovered in 12 cases (40.00%), improved in 10 cases (33.33%) and not improved in 08 cases (26.66%). Totally where as 12 cases showed recovered with constitutional homoeopathy remedies. This proving, the clinical utility of homoeopathic remedies in the management of type 2 diabetes mellitus. Further progress of the disease was arrested. Patients created general feeling prosperity.

The null hypothesis formulated in the beginning of the study " Homoeopathic medicines may not be helpful in the management of type 2 diabetes mellitus" is rejected and the alternative hypothesis homoeopathic medicines is helpful in the management of type 2 diabetes mellitus" from statistical analysis of the cases is accepted.

1. Christopher H, Edwin RC (1999). Davidson's principal and practice of medicine. 18th edition. Churchill living stone.pp.471-477.

2. Bishnu chowdhury (2016). Diabetes mellitus: A comparative study as per ayurvedic and modern classics. *Int J Res Ayu Phar*; 7(1):30-32.

3. Banerjee DD (1998). The glimpses of history of medicine. Reprinted, B. Jain publisher pvt. Ltd, New Delhi.pp.4-9.

4. Rawaa ali rahmat, Ali shalash sultan (2017). The effects of type 2 diabetes mellitus on the levels of testosterone, estradiol, gonadotropins and retinol binding protein 4. *Int J Adv Bil Res*; 7(2):404-410.

5. Ahmed AM (2002). History of diabetes mellitus. *Sau Med J*; 23(4):373-378.

6. American Diabetes Association (2009). Diagnosis and classification of diabetes mellitus. *Diabetes care*; 32(1):62-67. Doi: 10.2337/dc09-s062.

7. Robins, cotran ND (2011). Pathological basis of disease.8th edition. Elsevier. pp. 27.

8. Banister HL, Berry MM, Collins P, Dyson M, Dussek EJ (1996). Greys anatomy.38th edition, Churchill Livingstone publishers, Edinburgh. pp.1790-95.

9. Tortora GJ, Derickson B (2006). Principles of anatomy and Physiology.11th edition, John wiley and son's publishers.pp.916-918.

10. Munjal YP, Agarwal AK, Gupta P (2012). Association physician of India text book of medicine, vol-2.8[th] edition, A.P.I., Mumbai. pp. 1042.

11. Newsholme EA, Dimtriadis G (2001). Integration of biochemical and physiologic effects of insulin on glucose metabolism. *Exp Cli End Dia*; 109(2):122-134.

12. Mitrou P, Maratou E, Dimtriadis G (2011). Insulin effects in muscle and adipose tissue. *Diab Res Cli Pract*; 93(1):52-59.

13. Kumar p, Clark M (2005). Clinical medicine. 6th edition, Elsevier saunders publication. pp. 978-983.

14. A.P.I. Text book of medicine.9th edition, vol-2. Association of physician of India. pp. 397-402.

15. krishnadas KV (2008). Text book of medicine. 5th edition, Jaypee brother's medical publisher pvt. Ltd. pp. 546-555.

16. Harold E Lebovitz (1984). Etiology and pathogenesis of diabetes mellitus. *Elsevier*; 31(3):521-530.

17. Karen M, Kostick (2012). Coding diabetes mellitus in ICD-10-CM: improved coding for diabetes mellitus. Complements present medical Science. *J AHIMA*; 83(5):56-58.

18. Malik mumtaz (2000). Gestational diabetes mellitus. *Mala J Med Sci*; 7(1):4-9.

19. Zubin P (2018). Definition, classification and diagnosis of diabetes, prediabetes & metabolic syndrome. *Can J Diab*; 42:10-15.

20. Guyton AC (2006). Text book of medical physiology.11th edition, Elsevier saunders, Pennsylvania. pp. 972-975.

21. Mohan harsh (2002). Text book of pathology. 4th edition, Jaypee brother medical pvt. Ltd, New Delhi. McGraw Hill. pp.29.

22. Fauci, braumwald, kasper (2012). Harrison principal of internal medicine, vol-2, 18th edition, McGraw Hill, New York: pp.2968-2975.

23. Lawrence MT, Stephen JM, Maxine AP (2005). Current medical diagnosis and treatment. 44th edition, Lange text books. pp. 1157-1195.

24. Ramachandran A, latha E (1998). Evaluation of the use of fasting plasma glucose as a new diagnostic categories for diabetes in Asian Indian population. *Diab Care*; 21:666-667.

25. Michael EB, lei xuan, ethan A (2015). Random blood glucose: A robust risk factor for type 2 diabetes. *J Cli End Met*; 100(4):1503-1510.

26. Joycel baird, leslie JP Duncan (1995). The glucose tolerance test. *Pos Med J;* 35(403):308-314.

27. Scblienger JL (2013). Type 2 diabetes complication. *Press Med*; 42(5):839-848.

28. Campbell NP, Smith D, Anthony, Peters JT (2009). Biochemistry illustrated.5th edition. Elsevier Churchill Livingstone publications. Pp. 148-152.

29. Christos K, piperi C, fred Harris (2007). Type 2 diabetes mellitus and cardiovascular risk factors: current therapeutic approaches. *Exp Clin Cardio*; 12(1):17-28.

30. Martin M Nentwich, Michael wulbig (2015). Diabetic retinopathy- ocular complication of diabetes mellitus; 6(3):489-499.

31. Said G (2007). Diabetic neuropathy- A Review. *Nat Clin Pract Neur*; 3(6):331-340.

32. Juliana casqueiro, alves c, Janine (2012). Infection in patients with diabetes mellitus: A review of pathogenesis. *Ind J Endo Me*; 16(1):27-36.

33. Ripsin CM, Kang H, Urban RJ (2009). Management of blood glucose in type 2 diabetes mellitus. *Am Fam Phy*; 79(1):29-36.

34. Faas A,Schellevis FG, Van eijk JT (1997). The efficacy of self monitoring of blood glucose in NIDDM subjects. A critical based literature review. *Diab Care;* 20(9):1482-1483.

35. Thomas nihal (2008). Diabetic foot care. *Christian med J India*; 23(3):29-32.

36. Bennion LJ, grundu SM (1997). Effects of diabetes mellitus on cholesterol metabolism in man. *N Eng J Med*; 296(24):1365-1371.

37. Hiroshi K (2001). Guidelines for diet control in diabetes mellitus. Asia Med J; 44(2):57-63.

38. Sheri RC, Richard R (2010). Exercise and type 2 diabetes. *Diab Care*; 33(12):147-167.

39. Peter B, Anselm KG, Evelin D (2012). Oral antidiabetic treatment in type 2 diabetes in the elderly. Balancing the need for glucose control and the risk of hypoglycemia. *Card Diab*; 11(122):1-9.

40. James RL, Rachele B (2013). Insulin therapy in type 2 diabetes mellitus: A practical approach for primary care physicians and other health care professionals. *J Am Osteo Ass*; 113(2):152-162.

41. Ghosh K (2018). Diabetes mellitus: Homoeopathic approach. *Int J res Hom*; 7(4):184-185.

42. Ganong FW (2005). Text book medical physiology.22nd edition, International publisher. pp. 336-354.

43. Morgan W (1996). Diabetes Mellitus. reprinted edition. B. Jain publisher pvt. Ltd, New Delhi. pp. 94-97.

44. Herbert A Roberts (1999). The principal and art of cure by homoeopathy. Indian books and periodicals publishers, New Delhi. pp. 242-244.

45. Shankaran R (1999). The spirit of homoeopathy. 4th edition. Homoeopathic medical publisher pvt. Ltd. New Delhi. pp.57, 93-95.

46. Hahnemann SF (1998). Organon of medicine.6th edition. B. Jain Publisher pvt ltd., New Delhi. 233-235.

47. Hughes R (2001). The principal and practice of homoeopathy. Reprint edition. B. Jain publisher pvt ltd, New Delhi. pp. 628-630.

48. Choudhury (2005). Indications of Miasm. 2nd edition. B. Jain publisher pvt. Ltd, New Delhi. pp .13-34.

49. Deway AW (2002). Practical homoeopathic therapeutics. Reprint edition. Indian books and periodical publishers, New Delhi. pp. 68.

50. Farrington AE (2008). Clinical Materia Medica.4th edition. B. Jain publisher pvt. Ltd, New Delhi. pp .530.

51. Dubey SK (1998). Text book of materia medica. 3rd edition, part-II, Calcutta book and allied pvt ltd. pp.36.

52. Lilienthal saamuel (2006). Homeopathic therapeutics. Reprinted edition. B. Jain publisher pvt. Ltd, New Delhi. pp .288-292.

53. Dubey SK (1996). Text book of Materia Medica, Part II. Books and allied pvt. Ltd, Calcutta. pp. 55-56.

54. Patil JD (2008). Ground study in Homoepathic Materia Medica. Reprint edition. B. Jain publisher pvt. Ltd, New Delhi. pp .276-280.

55. Carry W George (1996). The bio chemic system of medicine. Reprint. B. Jain publisher pvt. Ltd, New Delhi. pp. 192-193.

56. Boeric William (2002). New manual of homoeopathic Materia Medica. 9th edition. Reprint edition. B. Jain publisher pvt. Ltd, New Delhi. pp. 1091-1108, 606,636.

57. Cowperthwaite CA (1998). A text book of Materia Medica and therapeutic. B. Jain publisher pvt. Ltd, New Delhi. pp. 374-417.

58. Burt HWM (2005). Physiological Materia Medica. 3rd edition. B. Jain publisher pvt. Ltd, New Delhi. pp .386-396.

59. Mathur KN (2008). Diabetes mellitus its diagnoses and homoeopathic treatment. Reprint edition. B. Jain publisher pvt. Ltd, New Delhi. pp .62.

60. Phatak SR (2012). Concise repertory to the dictionary of Materia Medica. 4th edition. B. Jain publisher pvt. Ltd, New Delhi. pp .192.

61. Clark JH (2001). Clinical repertory to the dictionary of Materia Medica. Reprinted edition. B. Jain publisher pvt. Ltd, New Delhi. pp .1173.

62. Boericke Osscar (2002). The clinical repertory. 9th edition. B. Jain publisher pvt. Ltd, New Delhi. pp. 828.

63. Boger CM (1997). Boeninghausens characteristics Materia Medica and repertory with word Index. Reprint edition. B. Jain publisher pvt. Ltd, New Delhi. pp .622.

64. D Schroyens Frederick (2001). Synthesis repertorium homeopathicum syntheticum. Reprinted. B. Jain publisher pvt. Ltd, New Delhi. pp .1924-1925.

65. Allen Timotsy Field (2010). Boeninghausen's therapeutic pocket book. Reprint edition. Indian book periodical publishers, New Delhi. pp. 99,145,234.

66. Boger CM (2011). Boger boenninghausen's characteristics & repertory. B. Jain Publisher pvt. Ltd, New Delhi. pp. 955.

67. Kent JT (1998). Kent's Repertory with word Index. 6th American edition. B. Jain publisher pvt. Ltd, New Delhi. pp. 691.

GRAPH - 1: COLUMN GRAPH SHOWING NUMBER OF CASES ACCORDING TO AGE

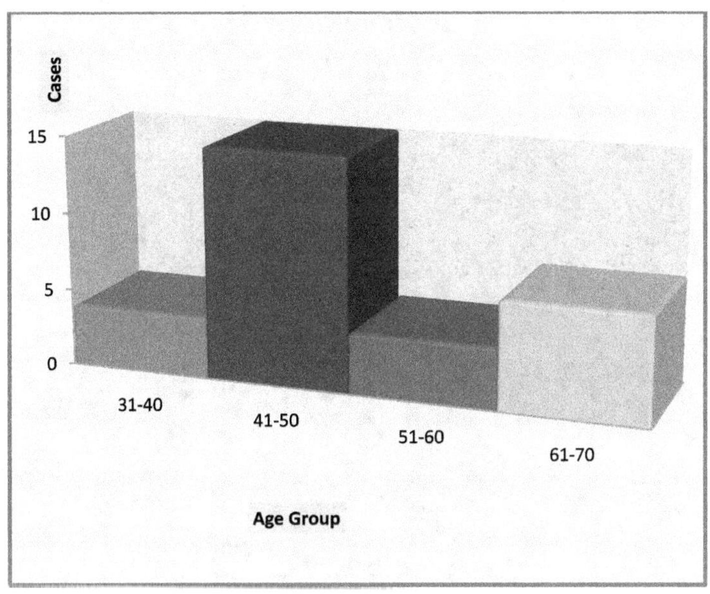

GRAPH - 2: COLUMN GRAPH SHOWING NUMBER OF CASES ACCORDING TO SEX

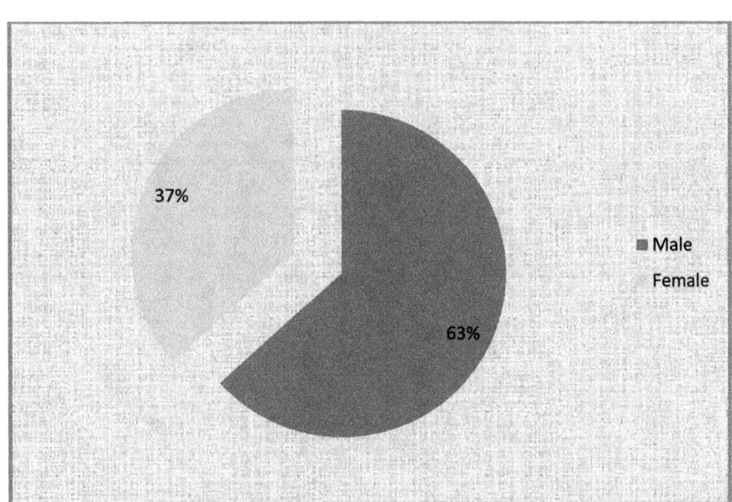

GRAPH - 3: COLUMN GRAPH SHOWING NUMBER OF CASES ACCORDING TO OCCUPATION

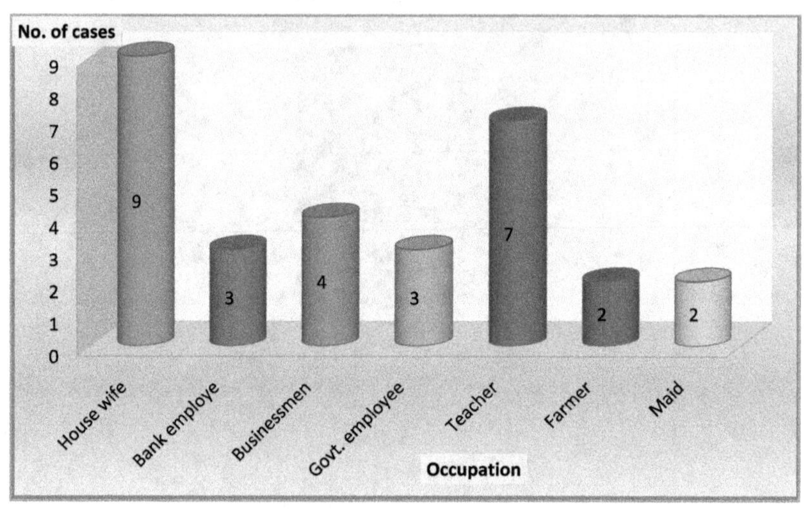

GRAPH - 4: COLUMN GRAPH SHOWING NUMBER OF CASES ACCORDING TO PHYSICAL COMPLAINTS

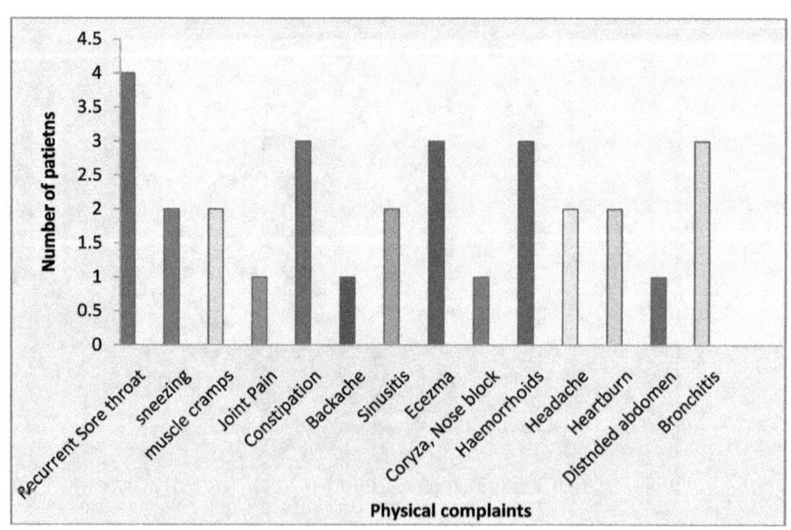

GRAPH - 5: COLUMN GRAPH SHOWING NUMBER OF CASES ACCORDING TO PAST HISTORY

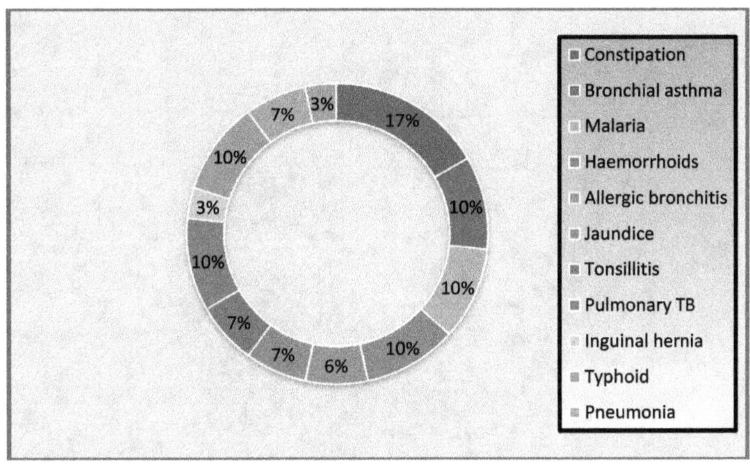

GRAPH - 6: COLUMN GRAPH SHOWING NUMBER OF CASES ACCORDING TO FAMILY HISTORY

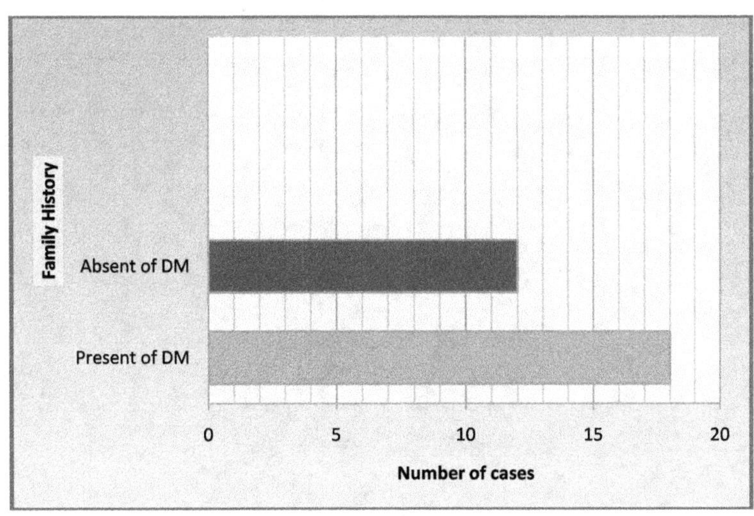

GRAPH - 7: COLUMN GRAPH SHOWING NUMBER OF CASES ACCORDING TO PRESCRIBED REMEDIES

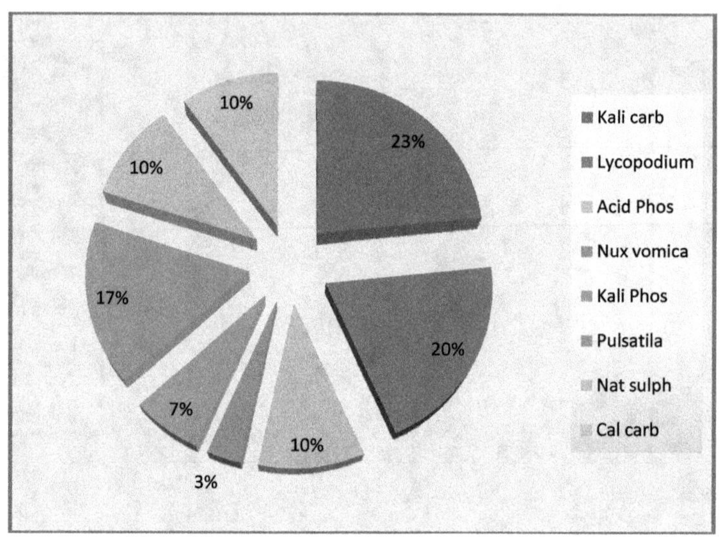

GRAPH - 8: COLUMN GRAPH SHOWING NUMBER OF CASES ACCORDING TO MIASMATIC BACK GROUND

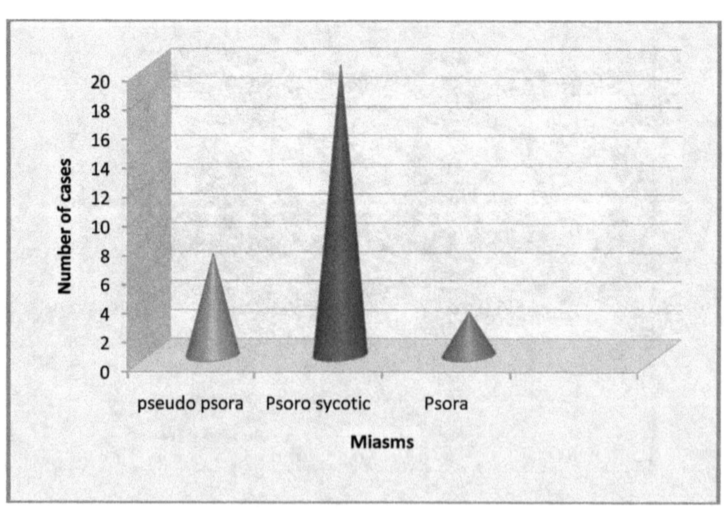

**GRAPH - 9: COLUMN GRAPH SHOWING NUMBER OF CASES
ACCORDING TO RESULTS**

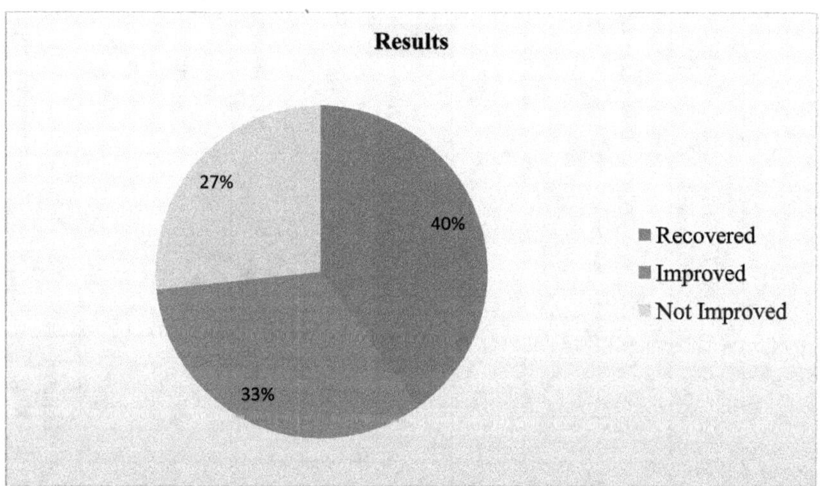

MASTER CHART

Case No	Name	Age/Sex	Occupation	Presenting Complaints	Past History	Family History	Predominating Miasm	Remedy	Results
1	LB	55/F	House Wife	GW,LMP, IFU	TP	M- Asthma	Psoro - Syphilitic	Calc carb	Improved
2	RSB	63/M	teacher	SE,SD,TLR, IB&S	AST	F-HTN	Psoro - Syphilitic	Nat sulp	Improved
3	SD	38/F	House Wife	BLL,GW, DSW	HRN	F-Asthma	Psoro – Syphilitic	Calc carb	Not Improved
4	YSB	50/M	Business man	IT,PP,IFU	HRN	F-Asthma	Psoro - Syphilitic	Kali carb	Improved
5	BSM	56/M	Govt. Employee	GW,BOV, DS, IT	HR	M –HTN	Psoro - Syphilitic	Nat sulph	Not Improved
6	MSP	33/F	Maid	IFU,DS,GW-L	TP	F-Asthma	Psoro - Syphilitic	Ac Phos	Improved
7	SAK	43/F	House Wife	GW,IH,IFU, DS	CP	F –DM	Psoro - Syphilitic	K carb	Improved
8	CJS	64/M	Business-man	IFU,GW,CLA	HR	M – DM	Psoro - Syphilitic	Ac Phos	Not Improved
9	SMR	68/M	Govt. Employe	DSW,GW, IB&S,TLR	NS	M – DM	Psoro - Syphilitic	Lyco	Improved

10	SSC	41/M	Bank Employee	PP,GW,IFU, SNZ, TLR	FT	F-HTN	Pseudo psora	Puls	Not Improved
11	AAG	47/M	Bank Employee	IFU,GW ,BOV, HS	SPT	F - HTN	Pseudo psora	Nux-Vom	Improved
12	MSP	47/M	Bank Employee	GW,IFU, DS, DSW	FT	M – DM	Pseudo psora	Kali Carb	Recovered
13	MDK	38/M	Teacher	HS,GDD, GW, IFU,PP	JD	M – HTN	Psora	K carb	Improved
14	LBK	68/F	House Wife	WLE,GW,DS	RC	F – DM	Pseudo psora	K carb	Recovered
15	NAJ	66/F	Maid	RMU,PB,IFU	FU	M – DM	Pseudo psora	Lyco	Not-Improved
16	PBH	47/F	House Wife	NOF,NHW, PP, TLR	JD	M – DM	Psoro - Syphilitic	K Carb	Improved
17	VSV	46/F	Govt Employee	SE,BLL,IH,PP	CKN	M/F – AST	Psoro - Syphilitic	Cal carb	Not-Improved
18	MRG	65/M	Teacher	PE,PP,IFU,GW	TP	F – DM	Psora	Lyco	Improved
19	NHP	45/M	Teacher	IT,UR,SNZ, IFU, DS	TP	M – HTN	Pseudo psora	Nat sulph	Not Improved
20	BGB	58/F	House Wife	DS,GW, IFU, CLE	GS	F – DM	Pseudo psora	K Carb	Recovered

21	JST	42/M	Business man	LOW,GW, RMU,IT, IFU, DSW	TP	M – DM F-HTN	Psoro - Syphilitic	Lyco	Recovered
22	NAJ	36/F	House Wife	GDD,BOV, GW,IR,PP	CKN	F - HTN M – DM	Psoro - Syphilitic	K Phos	Not Improved
23	AHH	58/M	Business man	BS,IT,PP,IFU	JD	M – DM	Psoro - Syphilitic	Puls	Recovered
24	UKT	48/M	Teacher	SD,IFU,PP, IB&S	NS	M – DM	Psoro - Syphilitic	K Ph	Recovered
25	SRS	46/F	House Wife	CLE,IFU, GW, DSW	TP	F – DM	Psoro - Syphilitic	Puls	Recovered
26	JK	48/M	Shop keeper	SD,IT,PP, DS, GW	TP	F&M - DM B&S – DM	Psoro - Syphilitic	Lyco	Recovered
27	RPG	49/F	House Wife	GDD, PP GW,IT	RC	M – DM	Psoro - Syphilitic	Puls	Recovered
28	SGP	46/M	Farmer	PP,GW- LL,IT,DS	MLR	M/F – AST	Psora	Ac Phos	Recovered
29	RTR	48/F	Teacher	CLE,GW,IT, DS	FU	F – DM	Psoro - Syphilitic	Puls	Recovered
30	STM	69/F	Teacher	RMU,SE, LMP, IT	TP	F - HTN M – DM	Psoro - Syphilitic	Lyco	Recovered

CASE NO 1: Mrs. LB, female, 55 years, married, house wife, presented with generalized weakness[++], lack of muscular power in both the extremities, increased frequency of urine 2-5/4-5 D/N with dryness of mouth since 2 years, on allopathic medication. Associated with headache and pain in the lumbar region since 2 months, with increased hunger & desire for sweets[++].she is very irritable, religious, hurries up doing any work. P/H Typhoid 5 years back. H/O: father DM mother Asthma. FBS 137mg/dl, PPBS 193mg/dl. **REMEDY** calc carb   **RESULT**: improved.

CASE NO 2: Mr.RSB male 63 years teacher presented with skin eruptions on right leg since 10 years, with presence of flakes, itching and burning sensation of skin, dark discoloration, rough, dry scaling of the skin itching < winter rainy season, cold air, evening ,brinjaal > warm application with k/c/o diabetic since 3 years under allopathic treatment .RBS 254mg/dl. Associated with thirstlessness, aversion for curd [++], patient prefers to be alone, always gloomy, low spirited and melancholic/H Asthma. F/O: father DM and mother asthma.

REMEDY: Nat Sulph . **RESULT**: Improved.

CASE NO 3: Mr. SD female 38 years, married, house wife. Presented with boil over leg which was not healing, generalized weakness with pain in both the knee joints <morning, sitting > warm application , k/c/o diabetic, under allopathic medication .RBS 188 mg/ml. associated with desire for sweets increased frequency of micturation. P/H: Hernia. F/H: father asthma. She is very restless, weeps while narrating her symptoms.

REMEDY: calc carb   **RESULT**: Not Improved.

CASE NO 4: Mr.YSB male 50 years businessman presented with dryness of lips and throat, sensation of vertigo < standing up , changing posture, > sitting, diagnosed as DM and on allopathic medicines associated with pain and numbness of left shoulder joint < hanging position > bending hand, .thirst increased 3-6 ltre /day desire for salty things profuse perspiration, increased frequency of urination. Patient is anxious, emotionally sensitive to bad news and disappointment. H/O: hernia. F/H: father asthma. FBS: 180mg/dl PPBS -300 mg/dl. **REMEDY**: kali carb

RESULT: Improved.

CASE NO 5: Mr. BSM, male, 56 years, govt employee, presented with generalized weakness , blurring of the vision, burning sensation in throat associated with sour eructation distension of the abdomen flatulency, increased thirst ,disturbed sleep. Patient is melancholic despondent, depressed, low spirited and disgust of life. P/H: Hemorrhoids. F/O father DM and mother HTN. RBS: 270mg/dl

REMEDY: Nat sulph **RESULT:** Not Improved.

CASE NO 6: Mrs. MSP, 33 years, female, widow, maid. Presented with profuse urination at night, Disturbed sleep & pain & weakness in lower extremities since 1 year associated with increased thirst & aversion for spicy food. She is very mild & depressed P/H Typhoid. F/H: father asthmatic, mother healthy. RBS.198 mg/dl **REMEDY:** Acid Phos **RESULT:** Improved.

CASE NO 7: Mrs. SAK, 43 yrs, female, married, house wife, presented with generalized weakness profuse Urination, increased hunger associated with both mental and physical fatigue / lethargy and disturbed sleep. Gets anger easily, irritable and wants company. P/H Chickenpox 5 years back. F/H Father is diabetic and RBS: 267 mg/dl. **REMEDY**: kali carb **RESULT:** Improved.

CASE NO 8: Mr. CJS, 64yrs, male, married, business man, presented with sour eructation's with Burning in the sternal region sensation of nausea with frequent urination 2-6/ 2-3 Times D/N, generalized weakness associated with complete loss of appetite desire For meat. Patient is very anxious due to family stress, confused always. RBS: 187 mg/dl. P/H: of Hemorrhoids 7yrs back. F/H: Mother DM

REMEDY: Acid Phos **RESULT:** Not Improved.

CASE NO 9: Mr. SMR, 68 years, male, married, govt employee presented with Itching and Burning sensation along with whitish discoloration in the scrotum. Sensation as if ants Crawling over the soles with generalized weakness associated with desire for sweets[++], Spicy food patient is thirst less with hard bowel movements, patient is very melancholic Prefers to be silent do not prefer company highly confident[++], restless[++], dominating+, RBS-198mg/dl. P/H nothing significant H/o: Mother was diabetic.

REMEDY: Lycopodium **RESULT:** Improved.

CASE NO 10: Mr.SSC, 41yrs, Male, Married, bank employee, presented with Profuse Perspiration and generalized weakness all over the body Diagnosed as diabetic 2yrs back, on regular medication associated with cold and coryza with Sneezing <early morning with running nose P/H: undergone surgery for Fistula. F/H: Mother diabetic and Father is HTN. Associated with Thirstlessness with desire for spicy food patient is very sentimental[+++] desires company, weeps easily wants consolation and irritable[+] RBS: 176mg/dl, **REMEDY:** Pulsatilla, **RESULT:** Not Improved.

CASE NO 11: Mr. AAG, 47yrs, Male, Married, Bank Employee presented with generalized weakness[++], blurring of vision, frequent urination 4-6/ 3-5 times D/N since 2- 3yrs, associated with sour eructation, Pain in the right hypochondriac region. Desire for meat, bowels are constipated patient is irritable, desires company does not prefer consolation very impatience haughty in nature. RBS: 215mgs/dl, P/H: Septicemia of lower extremities 3 yrs back. F/H: Father Hypertension Mother Diabetic.

REMEDY: Nux -vomica **RESULT:** Improved.

CASE NO 12: Mr.MSP 47 years male, married, bank employee presented with generalized weakness, frequent urination 7-8/3-4 D/N since 3 years with P/H Fistula and F/H mother Diabetic father died of hepatic disorder. Associated with desire for Sweets, aversion for Spicy, sleepless nights. Patient is generally anxious by nature[++], sentimental, desire for company, fear of crowd. RBS -250mg/dl.

REMEDY: kali carb **RESULT:** Recovered.

CASE NO 13: Mr. MDK 38 years male, married, teacher. Presented with passage of hard stools with giddiness, feels tired all the time diagnosed as diabetic since last 2 years on regular allopathic medication. P/H: jaundice. F/H mother DM. Associated with increased hunger and thirst for large quantities of water, profuse perspiration. Patient is irritable[++], weak memory[++], religious. RBS: 190mg/dl.

REMEDY: Kali carb, **RESULT:** Improved.

CASE NO 14: Mr.LBK. 68 years aged female, house wife presented with pain in the abdomen and generalized weakness, disturbed sleep,weakness of lower extrimities since 2 years. K/C/O DM on irregular medication and insulin injections. P/H Renal calculi. F/H father DM. Associated with restlessness, irritability, desires company, anxiety about future and health. RBS -170mg/dl.

REMEDY: Kali carb **RESULT**: Recovered.

CASE NO 15: Mrs.NAJ 66 years aged, female, maid. Presented with recurrent mouth ulcers and painfull boils around the edges of the angle of the mouth since 2 years. K/C/O DM on irregular medication and insulin injections. P/H: hysterectomy for fibroid uterus. F/H mother DM. Associated with desire for sweets thirst less 1 litre/day, scanty perspiration hot patient. Dominating in character[++], very timid at night, still wants to be alone. RBS: 210mg/dl.

REMEDY: Lycopodium **RESULT**: Not Improved

CASE NO 16: Mrs.PBH 47 years aged female, house wife presented with numbness of the foot, non healing wound over the right foot since 2 years. K/C/O DM on allopathic medication. P/H: typhoid and pneumonia. P/H: jaundice. F/H father died of CA throat and mother is diabetic. Associated with thirstlessness[++], profuse perspiration desire for fried items, spicy food. Patient is anxious[++], religious[++], weeps easily+, wants company RBS – 217 mg/dl.

REMEDY: Kali carb **RESULT**: Improved.

CASE NO 17: Mrs.VSV female 46 years, married, govt employee presented with skin eruptions, boils over the left leg since 2 months K/C/O DM on regular allopathic medicines. P/H Chikungunya. F/H both father and mother is Ast. Associated with increased hunger, desire for boiled eggs++, milk. Aversion for fatty food .profuse perspiration. Mentally the patient is confused all the time, dullness and sluggishness, slow in everything, anxious about the future. FBS-360 mg/dl

REMEDY: Calc-carb **RESULT:** Not improved

CASE NO 18: Mr.MRG aged 65 years male, married, teacher presented with pustular Eruption on the neck , upper and lower extremities With generalized weakness since 6 months with known case of diabetes since 10 years .itching < exposure to sunlight . P/H: Typhoid. F/H father was DM and undergone bypass surgery. Associated with profuse perspiration increased urination up to 6-7/4-5 D/N. hard working person who dislikes company wants everything neat and clean, dominating. RBS: 197 mg/dl.

REMEDY: Lycopodium **RESULT:** Improved

CASE NO 19: Mr. NHP 45 years male, married, teacher presented with urticarial rashes, Coryza and sneezing < early morning, banana, dust > medication, and burning soles ++ K/C/O DM since 1 year. P/H Hernia operated 5 years back. P/H: Typhoid. F/H Mother is HTN. Associated with increased thirst desire for spicy food, milk++, aversion for sweets, increased urination, sleep disturbed. Patient had ailments from grief, very ambitious, intelligent, fastidious, courageous and creative. RBS-250 mg/dl.

REMEDY: Nat sulph **RESULT:** Not Improved.

CASE NO 20: Mrs. BGB 58 years female, married, housewife presented with sleeplessness since 2 years with great weakness of the lower limbs < night , pain in the calf muscles and lumbar region < motion > rest, cramps in the lower extremities. P/H   Gall stones. F/H father is diabetic. Associated with hard stool, desire for spicy food, increased frequency of micturition. Very talkative, weeping tendency, wants sympathy and company. Attained menopause 8 years back. RBS: 207 mg/dl.

REMEDY: Kali carb **RESULT**: Recovered

CASE NO 21: Mr. JST 42 years male, married, businessman presented with loss of weight of 4-5 kgs, generalized weakness, ulceration at the corner of the mouth, increased frequency of urination under allopathic medicines since 8 years. P/H typhoid F/H mother is healthy and father is HTN. Associated with desire for sweets, increased Thirst. Worried much about family issues, sleepless nights due to anxiety. RBS-196 mg/dl.

REMEDY: Lycopodium **RESULT**: Recovered.

CASE NO 22: Mrs. NAJ 36 years, female, married house wife presented with giddiness, Weakness and blurring of the vision, weakness even with slightest work [++], increased thirst, 4-5 litres day. P/H Chikengunya F/H mother healthy father diabetic. Associated with aversion to sweets, profuse sweating all over the body. Patient is mild and co operative. RBS: 191mg/dl.

REMEDY: Kali-phos **RESULT**: Not Improved.

CASE NO 23: Mr.AHH, 58 years, male, married, businessman. Presented with burning soles < cold, walking > increased thirst esp. at night, profuse perspiration, P/H jaundice and stroke few years back. P/H mother is HTN and father died of old age. Associated with aversion to sweet, increased frequency of micturition esp. at night. Patient is debilitated poorly built. RBS: 227 mg/dl.

REMEDY Puls **RESULT**; Recovered.

CASE NO 24: Mr. UKT 48 years male married, teacher presented with severe drowsiness, increased thirst, frequent urination, 2-5 liters/ day with sensation of heat all over the day. Itching and burning sensation all over the body, P/H nothing significant. F/H mother and father HTN, elder brother is diabetic. Increased thirst, dryness of mouth, disturbed sleep feels drowsy always, RBS: 192 mg/dl.

REMEDY: Kalli phos **RESULT**: Recovered.

CASE NO 25: Mrs. SRS. Female, 46 years married, house wife presented with cramps in the lower extremities < night, profuse urination, generalized weakness. under allopathic medication. P/H typhoid twice at the age of 24 and 31.F/H mother and sister diabetic father healthy. Great desire for sweets. FBS: 170mg/dl.

REMEDY: Puls **RESULT**: Recovered.

CASE NO 26: Mr. JK, 48 years, male, married, shop keeper/farmer. Complaints are severe drowsiness & weakness < evening, on little exertion, motion > warm, lying down, rest. Dryness of mouth. P/H typhoid F/H father, mother, brother, sister is diabetic. Thirst is 2-5 liter/ day, desire for sweet, profuse sweating, increased frequency of urination at night, sleeplessness. Mentally the patient is afraid to be alone, sadness in morning, loss of self confidence, hurried when eating, amelioration by uncovering. FBS: 170 mg/dl, PPBS: 200 mg/dl

REMEDY: Lycopodium **RESULT**: Recovered.

CASE NO 27: Mrs. RPG, 49 years, female, married, housewife. Presented with pulling type of pain in the lower limbs < exertion[++], cold weather, morning, > warmth. Diagnosed as diabetic 1 year back after having giddiness and weakness all the body 1 year back. Under allopathic and ayurveda medicines. P/H Renal calculi 5 yrs back operated. F/H father is diabetic mother is healthy. Associated with unquenchable thirst at small intervals, desires spicy food, profuse perspiration, cannot able to stand for long time. Very obstinate, irritable, does not prefer company. RBS: 172 mg/dl.

REMEDY: Puls **RESULT:** Recovered

CASE NO 28: Mr.SGP. 46 years, male, married, farmer. Presented with profuse perspiration over the palms and soles with great weakness of the lower half of the body since 2 years and diagnosed as diabetic year back, on allopathic medicines. P/H malaria when he was child. F/H father and elder bro diabetic. Associated with disturbed sleep, sleeps rarely 2-3 hrs, increased thirst for ice cold water, epigastric burning. Patient is cheerful+, confused +, anxiety and fear about the future++, fears to be alone+. RBS: 234mg/dl. **REMEDY:** Acid Phos **RESULT:** Recovered.

CASE NO 29: Mrs. RTR. 43 years, female, married, teacher. Presented with muscular cramps in the lower limbs < night with generalized weakness all over the body, pain comes suddenly, disturbed sleep. Diabetic since 8 years. Suffered with chikungunya 3 years back. P/H Fibroid uterus and lipomas operated F/H father DM mother healthy. Very sentimental had lots of grief and disappointments in life, aversion for company, wants sympathy, very talkative in nature. RBS:227 mg/dl.

REMEDY: Puls **RESULT:** Recovered

CASE NO 30: Mrs.STM. 69 years, female, teacher presented with recurrent mouth ulcers, skin eruptions, lack of muscular power. Diagnosed as diabetic since 2 years on regular medication. P/H: Thypoid, F/H: Mother and Father died due to old age. Associated with increased thirst for 3 to 4 liters / day. Desire for sour items, fried food. RBS: 296 mgs/dl.

REMEDY: Lyc . **RESULT**: Recovered.